In this inspiring book, Beverley always been the most powerfu discover the power of the perso set of words and stories that have shaped our lives and can redefine our future.

> **Michael Margolis**, CEO, Storied, and author of *Story 10x: Turn the Impossible Into the Inevitable*

Beverley takes the much-discussed topic of storytelling and makes it accessible, relevant and easy for the rest of us to do. Her method is simple but brilliant – by harvesting the key words from your life, you unlock your stories. Beverley's own words take us on a riotous and touching journey through her life. This book in my words? Heartfelt, inspiring, original and must-read.

> **Sarah Lloyd-Hughes**, founder and CEO of Ginger Leadership Communications and author of *How to Be Brilliant at Public Speaking*

In Your Own Words is an exceptional and truly accessible guide to bringing your stories – and life – to life. Beverley is a masterful story coach, taking you through a simple yet brilliant process that asks you to challenge limiting beliefs and step into an empowering mindset and heartset to unlock your storytelling potential. Beverley's book is a real life-changing, story-changing game changer.

> **Biba Binotti**, founder and CEO of Global Warriors Ltd

Beverley has opened up a portal to let each of us find our words and bust out of our limitations.

> **Archana Mohan**, chief operations and technology officer, Veritas Investment Partners

The whole process of working with Beverley has been transformative for me. Not only was I able to share my story, but I also felt both witnessed and seen. Beverley and her process gave me the confidence to start my journey of writing from my heart. I'm delighted that Beverley has written this book. It means that even more people can learn about Beverley and her storytelling talent.
    Zena Me, founder of Eldership for Leaders (community-ofelders.carrd.co)

Beverley shows us something very special: how to tell the stories of our lives in ways that create connection and meaning. She does that by doing it herself in the most beautiful way, showing us rather than telling us how this can happen. If you have ever wanted to be able to use the experience of your life to make a difference, this book is for you!
    Mary Ann Clements, co-chief executive and transformation officer, Action on Disability and Development

I had the privilege of working with Beverley on my story a few years ago. It helped to bring clarity around what defined me, mostly through uncovering unknown drivers and patterns. Understanding their origin helped me to put the pieces of my puzzle together. I am so happy to see that Beverley is now sharing her gift with a large audience via this book.
    Raymond Honings, transformational business coach, owner and founder of Seemotion BV

This is an inspiring, insightful and moving guide to unleashing the potential of your life narrative. Having worked with Beverley on my own story, I'm so glad she has written this book.
    Lesley Pyne, author of *Finding Joy Beyond Childlessness*

In Your Own Words

Unlock the power of your life stories
to influence, inspire and build trust

Beverley Glick

In Your Own Words
ISBN 978-1-915483-38-6 (paperback)
eISBN 978-1-915483-39-3

Published in 2024 by Right Book Press
Printed in the UK

© Beverley Glick 2024

The right of Beverley Glick to be identified as the author of this work has been asserted in accordance with the Copyright, Designs and Patents Act 1988.

A CIP record of this book is available from the British Library.

All rights reserved. No part of this book may be reproduced, stored in a retrieval system, or transmitted in any form or by any means, electronic, mechanical, photocopying, recording or otherwise, without the prior written permission of the copyright holder.

Contents

Foreword by Nick Williams ... 7
Introduction ... 11

Part 1: A life in words ... 23

1: First words ... 25

2: Childhood words ... 29

3: Teenage words ... 41

4: Early adult words ... 57

5: Midlife words ... 79

6: Wise words ... 103

7: Last words ... 135

Part 2: How to use your words ... 139

8: Putting it all together ... 141

Epilogue ... 153
Acknowledgements ... 154
Resources ... 155

*To my mum, Lucille, for her eternal sparkle;
to my dad, Bill, for his sensitivity and humour;
and to all the friends I've loved and lost.*

Foreword

Nick Williams

Two stories come to mind about the power of words in my own life, both from my teenage years. When I was 15, our English teacher, Mrs Jamieson, arranged for the class to watch Franco Zeffirelli's *Romeo and Juliet*. It was food for my soul; Shakespeare's words spoke to me deeply. Even though I didn't fully understand his language, there was a beautiful resonance that touched something in me.

Sadly, I also took on board the idea of love needing to be tragic, which took me a while to shake off. If I ever get to meet Mr Shakespeare in spirit, I will have words with him about that, but I will also thank him for the beauty of his language and the impact his words have had on me. Even though they were written hundreds of years ago, it was as if he had stretched his hand and his heart across time to connect with me personally.

My dad was a Methodist lay preacher, delivering sermons to local churches on a Sunday. He also had a love of words and language and if he heard something interesting, funny and wise on TV, the radio or in a magazine, he would capture it. Then he would add it to a collection he called his Gems of Thought and weave them into his sermons.

Sometimes he would respond to something I'd say that he'd found wise or humorous and write my words down, adding them to his Gems of Thought. I would subsequently find my own words quoted and attributed in his sermons. I loved it and found it massively validating. I have no doubt he helped me find my way to my own life in words as a speaker, writer, author, coach and mentor. I make my living from saying the right words to the right people at the right time. Even though Dad died in 2005, I still have his Gems of Thought today.

I have known Beverley for more than a decade. I often ask her what she thinks of an idea I have had. In every one of our conversations, her love of storytelling and self-expression has shone through. I once asked her how many words she thought she might have had published and you can read her response in the introduction that follows.

While language can be utilitarian, useful and serve a purpose, it can also be deeply personal. Words can move and touch a heart; they can heal; they can create a resonance through the energy behind them. Now, Beverley has written another 40,000 words. I think these are some of her best yet. She has written a beautiful and engaging book straight from her heart about her lived experience of particular words and her passion for language.

Most of all, I love the way that Beverley has made the words personal. She has taken words that we all know and use and has let us know what they have meant to her. I feel a sense of privilege being allowed to see inside her soul. I hope you feel that privilege too.

I love that she has been acknowledged as the first person to use the term New Romantic in print and am thrilled along with her at the way that the idea entered the global consciousness. And then there's the heavy burden that a single word can carry. For Beverley, it's the word stroke and the story of how her and her family's lives changed in an instant. I love the way that Beverley shows us how a single word can open up a whole new universe of possibilities for us: writer, artist, entrepreneur.

I love it when someone expresses something very personal to them and, barely realising it, they also touch on something that we can all relate to, something we all feel. It's that wonderful gift of stretching a hand from one heart to another, one mind to another, helping us, if only for a moment, to feel less alone and more connected. 'Oh, it's not just me! I am not alone, I am human.' Like Shakespeare, Beverley has reached her hand and heart across time and space.

I'm not sure she understands how beautifully she has expressed her life in words and therefore shown us the way to express ours. Beverley is a pro; it's what she does and, like most of us, it's not easy for her to see the power of what she is doing so clearly. And, in some ways, that's not her business. Her business is to follow her love of words, storytelling and writing and to share the fruits with us. We are the greater benefactors of her work.

Thank you, Beverley, for your gift of this book. It has inspired me. Read it and be touched and inspired yourself. Here's to millions more words to come from your hand and your heart.

Nick Williams, leadership coach and author of 19 books, including The Work We Were Born to Do *and* Pivotal Moments.

Introduction

I started writing this book when the world ground to a halt in the spring of 2020. At the time, I was taken aback by the speed at which the English language was evolving and everyone around me started adding unfamiliar words (such as lockdown) to their vocabulary. These words helped us navigate uncharted territory and shape a narrative about our Covid-stricken lives. I doubt there are many people in the UK who wouldn't be able to tell you a story about the word 'pandemic' – a story that couldn't have been told before March 2020.

The next leap in the evolution of the English language will no doubt be driven by artificial intelligence. In fact, I asked ChatGPT what impact AI will have on language and it told me it will have a significant impact on the way we communicate and consume content. It shared its concerns that machine-generated text could lead to a loss of originality and creativity in human language. So the way I see it is that humans need to raise their game, use more inventive language and tell stories in more ingenious ways. In the future, 'written by humans' might become an important mark of quality and authenticity.

However, no matter how much influence viruses and technology will have in the future, humans will always be swimming in story. As Christina Baldwin writes in her beautiful book *Storycatcher* (2007), 'We live in story like a fish lives in water. We swim through words and images siphoning story through our minds the way a fish siphons water through its gills. We cannot think without language, we cannot process experience without story.' We are storytelling animals, wired to make sense of the world in story form and use words as gateways into our lived experience.

I know only too well that words can be weapons or bringers of beauty. During my 40-year career as a professional writer and editor, I've lobbed more than a few word bombs but also painted wonderful word pictures. I began my adventures in print in the early 1980s, travelling the world as a music journalist, and finished that journey as a travel writer. I left journalism behind as it gradually migrated from newsprint to news websites, trained to be a human potential coach then took a career swerve into the spoken word – training leaders to become more authentic communicators and storytellers. And now, in addition to my work in the public speaking arena, I help leaders develop their thought leadership and write books that will burnish their reputations and boost their businesses.

I've enjoyed a lifelong love affair with the English language; the way words are used in writing and speech is important to me. But I'm not a linguist, a philologist or a novelist. As a former journalist and now as a developmental editor and writing coach, I understand that telling stories well can bring personal and professional benefits. I believe in choosing words carefully to convey precise meaning. I also believe in using language that's simple enough to be understood by your average Jo.

Before I started writing this book, my dear friend Nick Williams (author of multiple books as well as the foreword to this one) asked me how many words I've had published over the years. After doing a rough calculation, I came up with a conservative estimate: *two million*.

Two million words that I've been paid to write – to entertain, inform and educate.

Introduction

Two million words in the pages of long-extinct magazines, on the fish and chip paper of national newspapers and more recently in blogs.

Two million words – some of which, I hope, have touched people's hearts, given them an insight into creative minds, introduced them to new music, helped them gain clarity, changed their thinking, called them to action, made them laugh or cry – or at the very least influenced their holiday plans. I'm a word millionaire and it feels good; I'm still astonished that my published articles have been read by millions of people.

Having written all of these words about other people, places and events, I thought it was about time I wrote about my own life – something I'm definitely an expert in. So, inspired by psychologist Carl Rogers' maxim 'What is most personal is most universal' (1961), I've chosen to write about the words that have had (and are still having) the most memorable impact on me. My intention is twofold: to reflect on the story I'm currently telling about my life via the words that I deem influential and say something about who I am; and to demonstrate and model how your significant words can open doors into your most personal, powerful and meaningful stories.

The speakers and writers with whom I work often tell me they don't have any interesting stories to tell and even if they did, why would anyone be interested? And I always reply, 'There's no such thing as an ordinary life. We all have an extraordinary story to share. We are all complete one-offs.' So who are you *not* to tell your story? I want to know who you are, what makes you tick, your unique perspective. I want to read and hear your story. I don't want that story to stay hidden. I want to find myself in that story. I want to connect with you. I want to benefit from the wisdom of your experience.

As storytelling coach Jay Golden writes in his book *Retellable* (2017), 'Your story, in fact, is made up of many stories. And these stories carry your most critical insights and lessons, create profound connection, cultivate alignment… and guide audiences across barriers to actions they have never considered.' I agree with his claim that the ability to tell a good story is 'one of the most important skills you have as a change-maker, innovator or business leader'.

This book is for you if you're one of the following:

- **You're a business leader** who understands that storytelling is a powerful tool and wants to learn how to leverage personal stories to build trust, serve an audience or land a message.

- **You're a speaker, writer or author** who would benefit from identifying meaningful personal stories to use in talks, blogs, articles or books.

- **You're a 'midlifer'** who's interested in personal growth and would benefit from a reflective process that helps you look back on your life and make sense of your journey so far.

Even if you haven't quite reached midlife, you may well have arrived at a point where looking back on your life will benefit your personal and professional development. You're reaching the peak of your powers, so now is the time to reflect on your life story to figure out where you've come from and where you want to go next.

Why tell stories?

When you think of storytelling, it might conjure up bedtime fairy tales or cosy fireside anecdotes, both of which are important in their own way. But there's also an evidence-based value in telling stories. A surprising amount of research has been conducted into the neuroscience of storytelling. According to Princeton neuroscientist Uri Hasson, 'By simply telling a story [you] can plant ideas, thoughts and emotions into listeners' brains.' (Widrich 2012) This also applies to writing a story.

So how does this work? There's a phenomenon known as neural coupling, which takes place in the brains of the teller and listener/reader. When you tell a story (in the spoken or written word), your brain synchronises with the brains of your audience, which is how you can plant ideas. It may sound creepy but it happens all the time! Hasson adds that 'a story is the only way to activate parts in the brain so that a listener turns the story into their own idea and experience'.

I appreciate the analogy referenced by neuroscientist David Eagleman on the Stanford podcast *Think Fast, Talk Smart* about the climactic moment in *Star Wars: A New Hope* when Luke Skywalker aims his proton torpedoes into the vent shaft of the Death Star: 'It's not easy to infect the brain of another person with an idea; it can be accomplished only by hitting the small, exposed hole in the system. For the brain, that hole is story-shaped.' (Stanford Business 2021)

Being immersed in a narrative also activates the brain's mirror neuron system. The listener/reader mirrors the emotions experienced by the characters in the story. And, according to psychologist Lani Peterson (2017), scientists are also discovering that when we're told a story, chemicals such as cortisol, dopamine and oxytocin are released. Why does this matter? Because if we're trying to make an idea stick, cortisol assists with formulating memories, dopamine keeps us engaged and oxytocin (the 'empathy chemical') helps us to build, deepen or maintain good relationships. If you need more evidence, Jennifer Aaker, a professor at Stanford University, states that stories are remembered up to 22 times more than facts alone (2019).

There's also a fascinating field of study around narrative identity theory, which explores the impact and benefits of framing your life in story form. In an interview, psychologist Dan McAdams said that we start to become 'historians of the self' in adolescence and this history changes and evolves from that point onwards (Mufarech 2022). We're constantly revising our story of self, influenced by what's happening in our lives and how we feel about ourselves at any given moment. And whatever story we're telling about our lives right now will give an indication of where we're heading in the future. McAdams sees life stories as 'psychological resources' that we use to help us make decisions and move forward in life.

Why I tell stories

The meaning of the word 'storytelling' and its evolution tells a story in itself. Storytelling was originally a recital of true events – an oral history, if you will. Before the advent of writing, it was the only way people could pass on their knowledge and wisdom. It was much later that it came to mean a fictitious narrative told for entertainment purposes. Then, in the late 1600s, when storytelling became a euphemism for lying, its fate was sealed. After that, storytelling itself couldn't be trusted and I believe that's why some of the business leaders I work with today are resistant to the idea of storytelling – they don't take it seriously or, worse, believe it undermines their credibility.

Let me state my case, unencumbered by dictionary definitions. I think of storytelling as the 'primal technology' – it's how we make sense of the world and have done since we lived in caves. We cannot *not* tell stories. We don't know who we are without storytelling. It's how we create meaning, connection and community. We can't exist without storytelling. As the author Jonathan Gotschall writes in his book *The Storytelling Animal* (2013), 'We are, as a species, addicted to story. Even when the body goes to sleep, the mind stays up all night, telling itself stories.'

I've written stories for many years but the act of storytelling has been a more recent adventure. When I met Mary Ann Clements (a fellow speaker, writer and advocate of the power of story) in 2012, we decided to launch a regular storytelling event in London called The Story Party. Our intention was to provide a platform for anyone who wished to share a personal story (on a given theme) with a caring and supportive audience – and public speaking experience wasn't required. In fact, some of the most moving stories shared at our events were told by people who had never spoken in public before – people who simply wanted to have their stories witnessed and honoured. We also heard stories that had never been shared before. The most powerful example of this for me personally was when my sister told a story. Having had this witnessed by the audience, she told me (and the other family members in attendance) that she would not disclose the experiences she talked about again. It was cathartic for her and deeply moving for the rest of us.

I believe that personal storytelling is an act of leadership that requires courage and vulnerability. It builds self-awareness and emotional intelligence and acknowledges our flawed humanity in all its glory. If we don't tell our story and tell it well, we're effectively denying others the wisdom and learning inherent in that story. Don't forget that when you have turned to dust, all that remains is the story people tell about you. And that's why it's important to take control of the narrative you leave behind. I'm inspired by the words of Richard Stone in *The Healing Art of Storytelling* (1996), 'At the end of our lives, after we have passed on, all that is left of us is our story. In a peculiar way, these stories are our ticket to immortality. Knowing that future generations will retell our stories liberates us into a realm of timelessness.'

So, I invite you to start exploring your story of self and building your 'psychological resources', as Dan McAdams terms them. The unique premise of this book is that it's all about using particular words to access your personal stories. This approach will allow you to focus on the *meaning* of those stories and what you've learned from them about yourself and your life. It also will help you to tell *lean* stories and avoid rambling tales filled with every small (and often superfluous) detail. Like dictionary definitions, all of the 'word stories' I've told in this book are concise and specific. So I'd like you to think of yourself as a lexicographer compiling a 'life dictionary'.

How to use this book

As you'll discover, compiling a life dictionary requires self-awareness and the ability to reflect. To demonstrate the process, I've hand-picked words that had particular significance for me at various stages of my life and written a short story about why. These are not the only words ever to have had an impact on me but they are the words that are still *actively* influencing me.

Words can hold meaning for you beyond the dictionary definition. They can boost your self-image but can also consume your energy and skew your self-image. That's why identifying your list of chosen words can play an important part in understanding yourself and what motivates you. Picking out words in this way also provides a shortcut to writing about your life story.

I invite you to use my words as triggers to find the words (and stories about those words) that are meaningful to you in a positive way as well as the words that are still holding you back. As you'll see as you read on, I found that certain stages in my life triggered more words than others and you may find the same. Don't feel constrained by the life stages that I've outlined, especially if you haven't yet reached midlife. Whatever your age, you can still follow the process and come up with your own stages of life.

I've included a list of prompts at the end of each chapter – questions to help you reflect more deeply on the words that have had the greatest impact on you. They may be words to treasure or words that are still playing on your mind. You may uncover entire narratives that are no longer fit for purpose or stories that align with your values and purpose that can make your speaking or writing more memorable.

I've also inserted several pauses for reflection along the way, which are intended to provide a running commentary on the process as I went through it, as well as more information about the key markers in a typical story structure and how you might thread your word stories into an overarching narrative (see Chapter 8 for more about how you might go about this). There are many varieties of story structure (book publishing resource Reedsy (2022) has a useful guide), but when it comes to autobiographical storytelling the simplest way of framing your story is to think of your life as a *journey* and yourself as the hero who has to overcome challenges and obstacles but meets mentors and helpers along the way.

Here are the key points in this type of story structure:

- **The inciting incident:** According to Reedsy (2021), the inciting incident is 'the event that ignites the story's plot and starts the protagonist's transformative journey'. This applies to non-fiction as well as fiction.

- **Progressive complications (rising action):** These are moments of conflict in the protagonist's life that become more challenging to deal with over time. They can have a positive or negative impact but always relate back to the inciting incident.

- **Crisis (or turning) point:** This is self-explanatory but there's at least one of these in a story, when the progressive complications culminate in a crisis of some kind for the protagonist. It's often the tipping point in a story that forces the protagonist to change and reveals their true character.

- **Climax:** This is the moment when the story reaches its highest point of tension or excitement and/or when the stakes for the protagonist are at their highest.

- **Resolution:** This happens after the climax of a story and resolves the conflict triggered by the inciting incident. The protagonist comes full circle and begins another story cycle.

Introduction

As you're still living your story, it won't have an ending as such but there will be complete story cycles within your journey. For example, even though my story continues, I can identify a resolution in my story so far. You may, as I did, experience several 'aha' moments as the words and stories start to reveal themselves. You may also reach a deeper understanding of your hidden motivations and limiting beliefs, which will help you reach a more satisfying resolution.

The key to crafting a meaningful story is to understand that it's about *transformation*. As a result of the hero/protagonist (in this instance, you) going on a journey, something changes. If nothing changes, it's not a meaningful story. You may experience a small change while writing about your chosen words but once you find the connections between them and piece together a complete narrative, that's when the transformation occurs. A fresh perspective might shift your mindset or behaviour and it will definitely increase your self-knowledge.

Many of the entries that follow are also informed by etymology – the study of the origin of words and how their meaning has changed throughout history. I often check the original meaning of a word because it adds a layer of depth to my intuitive process. I still have my dad's old *Collins Etymological Dictionary*, which he was first given at school in the 1930s; it reminds me that my enchantment with words goes all the way back to childhood. When your words bubble up, I recommend looking up their etymological roots. There are many free resources available online but I prefer the Online Etymology Dictionary, which I've used for the definitions of words included here. Following your intuition is the priority here but exploring the origins of a word may provide extra insight and help to explain why it holds significance for you.

I'd also recommend buying a lined notebook (with a hard cover) that you can dedicate to this process. All the prompts in the book are designed to be answered in longhand, not on a laptop, desktop or mobile device – although it's OK to use a notes app if a word or story comes to you when you don't have your notebook to hand. There's research to back this up. According to *Psychology Today* (Michelson Foy 2022), writing longhand can boost analysis and recall as well as creative flow.

Are you sitting comfortably?

Are you ready to take charge of your narrative and become the author of your own life? Before you begin, a word of warning: this process requires honesty and courage. If you find that any challenging emotions (anger, sadness, fear) consistently bubble up or you start to feel overwhelmed, please seek support from a qualified therapist or counsellor. But always remember that you're in control of what you choose to share – privately or publicly. If you're planning to share personal stories in written or spoken form, make sure they're *from your scars, not your wounds*, ie stories you have processed emotionally and extracted the learnings from rather than stories that are still emotionally raw. Choosing meaningful words to write about also enables you to be *selective* in what you share with others and to stay in control of your narrative.

Good luck and I'll meet you again at the end of this journey. I'll share more ideas about how to compile your life dictionary and what to do with your word stories in Chapter 8.

Part 1
A life in words

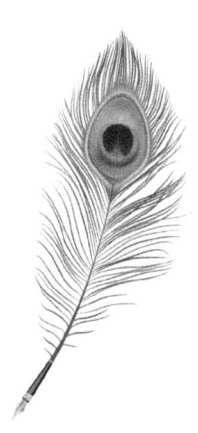

Chapter 1
First words

At the start of your life, months of baby babbling eventually result in the formation of recognisable words or word-like forms. Unlike last words, first words aren't deemed to be of cultural value and are rarely celebrated, except by doting parents. My favourite take on first words was recorded by anthropologist Nigel Barley, who observed in *The Innocent Anthropologist* (2012) that the Chamba people of Cameroon and Nigeria believe that the babbling of infants and of people affected by dementia is the language of the spirit world: 'The former have not yet forgotten it, the latter are resuming it, hence their affinity with each other.'

Once you've adopted your native tongue, you quickly learn the meaning of simple negative and affirmative words. But I do wonder about the impact of the language you hear but don't yet understand. The energy of these words may have instilled an instinctive feeling of being loved or alternatively a feeling of fear and dread. You'll never know – but perhaps you sense it at the deepest level of your being.

In common with many other babies of different nationalities, my first word described the person closest to me – the human being I depended on the most. I'm wondering… if you struggled to be understood as a baby, does that struggle continue throughout your life?

Mama

A few months before she died in September 2020 (at the grand old age of 93), I asked my mum (the amazing Lucille) to name my first intelligible word. She reckoned my debut was (the entirely unoriginal) 'Mama'. According to an article in *The Paris Review* (Erard 2019), Picasso's first word was 'piz' (Spanish for pencil) and Julie Andrews' was 'home' – both of which are much more intriguing first words and seem connected to what they'd end up becoming known for (Picasso for his art, Julie Andrews for playing the world's most famous nanny). However, Mum did add a little detail: as I was learning to form words, I'd always be pointing at something. I'd like to think that indicated I was curious from the word go. She also told me that I learned to speak early and quickly and I'm happy to own that story. A life in words beckoned…

Pause for reflection

If your mother, father or guardian is still alive, ask them about your first word. It may lead you to a story about your first steps into communicating and expressing yourself. It may even lead you to a key value, which may in itself prompt a story.

I'm so grateful I was able to ask my mother about my first word before she fell into cognitive decline. Even though millions of other people share 'Mama' as a first word, I found my own meaning in it, especially in the early signs of my curiosity. I've never stopped being curious and this allows me to create a positive self-narrative.

Here are a few prompts to help you reflect on your first word(s). Choose one that resonates with you, find a quiet space where you won't be interrupted and write down whatever comes into your mind. Don't overthink or edit it. Set a timer and write for at least five minutes without stopping. This is the best way to access your memory and unleash your creativity. If an unrelated story emerges, go with it anyway. There will be a connection somewhere. This is the process I have used to write about many of the words in this book and I've often been intrigued by what has emerged.

- Was your first word recorded and/or celebrated by your parents/guardian?
- Was it unusual, unique or memorable?
- What does that word mean to you now?
- Do you still carry that word with you?
- Does it bring back fond memories or difficult ones?

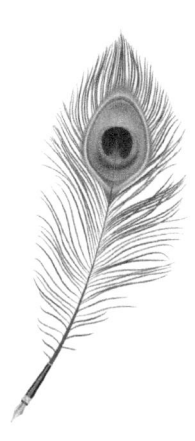

Chapter 2
Childhood words

In this chapter I'm referring to words that had an impact on you during childhood – words that were part of your family's vocabulary, words that shaped your early identity, words that shaped your outlook, words that still hold meaning for you from that time. My words explain a little about how I perceived and experienced the world around me as I was growing up in what was, for me, a comforting, innocent time before life started to get complicated. Your childhood may have been happy, unhappy or uneventful. Whichever way, words will be echoing through your mind that will conjure stories from your earliest years when you were learning to understand language and building your vocabulary.

Corners

This word was exceptionally meaningful to me in my formative years. It's a word that my mum came up with to describe my comforter – the original version of which was the rectangular tip of the sash on my soft, winceyette nightie. Being practical yet creative, Mum would later run up copies of these corners – an approximately 12 x 1 inch strip of seamed fabric – on her Singer sewing machine. For reasons I still can't explain, I comforted myself by tapping the corners of the fabric against the side of my nose. I remember it being exquisitely pleasurable – and I continued tapping until I was about eight years old. It was such a private experience that this is the first time I've ever written about it.

I've recently read some psychological theories around adaptive behaviour in children and it makes sense to conclude that what I did with my corners was a form of adaptive behaviour that helped to soothe me when I was feeling anxious or overstimulated.

I'm hoping that you had your own version of corners when you were a child, or at least something that had a special meaning for you – a pet name, a toy, an imaginary friend. Even now, if I think of the word corners it will always evoke that strip of fabric and never what the word means in everyday language. It's not a word I hear that often (who even talks about more than one corner?) but when I think about it, I'm a child again, feeling ever so slightly embarrassed that I did this weird tapping thing with a piece of cloth. However, it made me feel calm and contented, so who cares what anyone thinks?

I find it interesting that, if you tap the side of your nose with a finger, the gesture is understood to mean 'It's a secret' or 'Keep your nose out of my business'. I reckon many of us have a set of words with personal meanings, words that elicit memories that no one else will share. And I think that's one of the things that makes each of us unique – our own secret vocabulary.

Pause for reflection

When you're reflecting on your childhood words, trust whatever springs to mind. Don't judge what emerges. These words may or may not be part of your 'secret vocabulary', but if they are, they may have become so internalised that you haven't even considered sharing them or digging into their meaning until now.

When I reflected on my formative childhood word, what struck me was that it's a word that has many meanings but this one is unique to me. It gave rise to the insight that I have a rich internal world that I don't readily give people access to. I'm not an open book – at least, I haven't been until now – so that one word gave me access to a part of myself that I often keep hidden.

Before I go any further, it's worth mentioning that it's important to look for the 'gleaming details' in your word stories. This concept was coined by screenwriter Bobette Buster in her brilliant little book *Do Story* (2013). A gleaming detail is something that best captures and embodies the essence of the story – a specific moment or one that evokes the senses, for example, the soft, winceyette fabric that I found so comforting as a child.

Use the prompts at the end of this chapter to help you access words, sense memories and therefore stories from your early years that might give you and other people valuable insight into the way you think and feel now.

Sunshine

I could write a separate book about the lyrics that have had an impact on me over the years, but when thinking about my childhood words, my mind focused on a word that features in the lyrics of a song my mum used to sing to me when I was tiny. That song was 'You Are My Sunshine' – originally recorded in 1940 but subsequently covered by numerous artists, including Doris Day (in 1951) and Nat King Cole (in 1955). It was probably one of the later versions that hooked my mum to such an extent that she sang the chorus to me as a lullaby. I can't quote the lyrics (they're still under copyright) but the key words for me were about being her sunshine, how I made her happy and that I'd never know how much she loved me. Rather like my corners, I found solace in this song and it always sent me to sleep.

It was only in recent years that I pondered the meaning of the words, about how much I was loved and how I was the light of my mum's life. I'm sure my siblings were too – but I don't think she sang them this song. As a result, it was anchored into me pretty early on that sunshine = love, safety and contentment. There's something so pure about the word sunshine – it exudes boundless joy and exuberance. Sunshine is effervescent. It's the essence of life. The irony is that I burn easily in the sun but even that painful reality doesn't stop me from connecting with this word. There seemed to be a lot of it in my childhood.

Many, many songs have included sunshine in their lyrics. In recent times, the best known has been Katrina and the Waves' version of 'Walking on Sunshine', which was a hit in 1985. There's an irrepressible quality to that song (which

I have performed myself) that says everything you need to know about the word sunshine. I think everyone could benefit from more sunshine in their lives, both literally and metaphorically.

Night-night

And so we go from sunrise to sunset. When I was still small enough to be carried to bed in the rented flat in East Dulwich, London, where I was born in 1957, I'd insist on saying goodnight to an array of household objects – most notably the washing machine. My exact words ('night-night washing machine') were captured for posterity by my dad, who owned a reel-to-reel tape recorder and liked to use it to record amusing family moments. In hindsight, I'm surprised we even had a washing machine in those days. Perhaps that's why I singled it out for special treatment; such a modern, labour-saving device must have transformed my mum's life.

Even though night-night holds a meaning for me that's rooted in the 1950s, the expression dates back to the late 19th century, when it was used as a form of 'nursery talk' in place of 'good night'. I dropped the washing machine (figuratively, not literally) when I grew up but kept the 'night-night' and still use it if I'm staying with family members (often abbreviated to 'ni-night'). It belongs to my collection of expressions that make me feel cosy and safe. Many of us have them and I bet they rarely make it onto the page. I love the fact that they're so hush-hush. If you have one, what's your cosy word?

Gibberish

It's ironic that, for someone who's fascinated by the meaning of words, I'm also a big fan of nonsense. This is all my dad's fault. He had a surreal sense of humour that was directly influenced by the legendary radio comedy *The Goon Show*, starring Spike Milligan, Harry Secombe and Peter Sellers. Just like they did in the show, he would often make up gibberish that sounded a bit German and a bit Yiddish (not surprising, as his Jewish grandmother was Russian and didn't speak English). He would often say something like '*Vein blott kitroiluk in de cloils*' around the house, along with Goons catchphrases such as 'Needle nardle noo' and 'You rotten swine, you!' I had no idea what any of this meant but it didn't matter. I loved the fact that my dad could be this silly on a regular basis and it planted a seed in my young mind – if you can play with words, you can make people laugh. It also formed the foundation of my own sense of humour and paved the way for my love of *Monty Python's Flying Circus*.

Gibberish is, of course, a 'hindsight word'. It wasn't part of my childhood vocabulary but makes it onto my list because it sums up my dad's absurd sense of humour. It's also a genuinely silly word – so much sillier than nonsense. Interestingly, it dates all the way back to the 1600s, when it referred to rapid or inarticulate speech or talking in an unknown language. However, the word will always remind me of my dad during my halcyon childhood years when laughter would echo around our house in response to his made-up language. This is a good example of a word that has a particular meaning for me that isn't revealed by its dictionary definition or etymology. You may have words like this too.

Pause for reflection

My 'early years' words revolve around my parents. I'm struck by how comforting they still feel to me all these years later and what a happy household I lived in, one in which I felt nurtured and cared for. Your childhood words may be less comforting. Which words spring to mind when you think about your parents' influence and impact on you in your early life? Do they tell a different story – one that's a bit more painful to write? Or was yours an uneventful childhood? Even if you don't have any standout memories, there will be a word or words that have significance for you and give rise to a meaningful story.

Shy

I always used to describe myself as a shy child. It's true that I could be timid in the classroom but I was sociable in the playground. What upset me and set me back at primary school were the consistent comments on my school reports that I didn't participate in class discussions or put my hand up to answer questions. Even though I was a conscientious student, these remarks made me feel bad and wrong. Shy became a label that made me feel even less confident – and I wasn't that confident to begin with.

It was only years later, when I discovered that I was an introvert, that my apparent timidity and lack of participation started to make sense. Introverts tend not to speak up unless they've carefully thought through what they want to say. Because it takes them time to process their thoughts and feelings, they're unlikely to compete with an extrovert who likes to process their thoughts by speaking them out. That's why they're unwilling to play the 'hands up' game. Heard the old saying 'Sticks and stones may break my bones but words will never hurt me'? Well, for a sensitive introvert, that's simply not true.

I hope the education system has changed since I was at school. It's important to recognise the value of what young introverts have to offer and give them a safe space to express themselves. If they're labelled 'shy' they're likely to take it to heart and not fulfil their highest potential. I was rarely reluctant to participate and I certainly wasn't scared of people. Shy is not a helpful descriptor. Be careful if you choose to call somebody shy. They may struggle to get over it.

My understanding of being shy deepened when I took the Myers–Briggs Type Indicator personality test and came out as an INFJ – considered to be the rarest of all personality types. INFJs have advanced people skills but tend to be drained and overstimulated by too much social contact. They enjoy alone time but crave meaningful connection. So, call me quiet, call me withdrawn, call me reserved, call me self-contained but never call me shy.

After I wrote this entry, a friend alerted me to a book by the poet and philosopher David Whyte called *Consolations: The Solace, Nourishment and Underlying Meaning of Everyday Words* (2014). Whyte has selected a collection of words to reflect on in his deeply felt, poetic way. One of his chosen words is shyness and his take on it has helped me to reframe the meaning of shy. He writes: 'Shyness is the exquisite and vulnerable frontier between what we think is possible and what we think we deserve.' He reclaims it as a valuable way of approaching the new. That's how quickly you can reframe the meaning of a word so that it becomes more empowering.

Popular

It may seem incongruous to include the word popular immediately after shy but this is what it's like to be a sociable introvert. At around the age of six, I recall my form teacher asking the most popular person in the class to stand up. Without a second thought, I pulled back my chair and stood up. No one else did. First of all, what kind of request is that to make of young children? What message did that send? And second, it shows the lack of self-consciousness we often have at that age. I instinctively knew that I was the most popular child in the class. I was the kid who avoided cliques and connected with different friendship groups. Every single classmate I invited to my sixth birthday party – bar one, who desperately wanted to come but couldn't – attended.

Many years later, I read in the book *The Secret Language of Birthdays* (Goldschneider & Eiffers 1994) that my birthday is known as 'The Day of Popularity'. Apparently, those born on that day display a great need and capacity to be popular with their social set. Indeed, they wish to be admired and praised by those they care about. I can't disagree with that. There was, however, a downside to this, as I often crossed the line between popular and people-pleaser. Popular is from the Latin word meaning belonging to or accepted by the people; it came to mean well liked or admired much later. The same word would return later in my life and make an equally big splash…

Pause for reflection

The two previous words – shy and popular – allowed me to stop and think about words that you allow to define you when you're just beginning to work out who you are. These types of words can become labels that are hard to shake off as you approach adulthood and indeed you may carry them with you as you go through life. I pushed back on one of my 'labels' and embraced the other. Did you have a similar dynamic operating in your childhood? The value here is that such words might uncover a powerful narrative that your readers or listeners will be able to find themselves in. And in the words of Michael Margolis, one of my storytelling superheroes, in his book *Believe Me* (2009), 'Only when people can locate themselves inside the story will they truly belong and participate in your narrative.'

You're looking for words you've been carrying since you first understood what words were. Some of them might be words that you didn't use at the time. They might be words from your current adult vocabulary that encapsulate a particular childhood feeling or memory. You might also find, as I did with 'popular', that the same word will have a different meaning and/or impact at a different time in your life.

The following prompts are here to start you on your journey. As before, choose one (or two) that triggers an immediate response or memory, sit down and keep writing your answer for at least five minutes or until you run out of steam.

- *Are there words that 'labelled' you as a child?*
- *Are there words that can still strike fear into you?*

Childhood words

- *Are there words that evoke a feeling of warmth?*
- *Are there words that encouraged or wounded you as a child?*
- *Has your relationship with these words changed over the years?*
- *Did you have secret or made-up words as a child?*

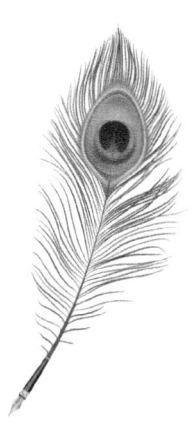

Chapter 3
Teenage words

Puberty: that period in your life when your skin becomes paper thin and any word or sentence can be perceived as a slight, an insult or a criticism. This is when you often hear words that wound, words you don't understand or words you fear. But you also use words that affirm your emerging identity and share words that are understood only by you and your circle of friends. Your teens are often the time when you start writing diaries that are for your eyes only. Words are committed to paper in an attempt to figure out who you are and what your place is in the world. I kept a diary for one year only – the year I left school at 18. Unfortunately, I wrote half of it in Pitman's shorthand, which I no longer understand. It's like an ancient text that I can't decipher! What follows are the words that have stuck with me from my teenage years – words that tell a story about my sensitivity as well as my resilience. Whatever your experience, you may find your teenage words are still occupying space in your consciousness.

Messy

On the whole, I was a studious teen – a fast learner in most subjects apart from maths (numbers were not my forte, even though I was in the top stream). My school reports were good to excellent, with most of my marks above a solid B+. But despite this consistency all the way through technical high school, the only mark and comment I'll always remember were those given to me by my domestic science teacher: 'C+ – messy worker.' My, what constructive feedback! Nothing about my ability to follow recipes or cook edible dishes. Nothing. Just *messy*.

Messy. Untidy. Confused. Chaotic. Dirty. Filthy. Grimy. I didn't want to have anything to do with any of these words. I didn't see myself in any of them.

I can honestly say that this word undermined my culinary confidence to such an extent that, to this day, I rarely cook from scratch. Messy is an example of a word that I spun into a narrative that affected my whole life. If you stop to think, you might have one of those word stories too.

The human brain has a significant bias towards the negative, so it's no surprise that we remember criticism more than encouragement. And it was even worse for a young introvert who was sensitive to criticism and didn't want to be thought of as untidy or disorganised – and definitely not dirty. Despite all the glowing remarks I received from other teachers over the years, this is the one that stuck because it was the lowest mark I ever received in all my years of schooling. When I think of that teacher now, I feel righteously indignant. How *dare* she be so dismissive. How *dare* she be so unsupportive. Fifty years later, the memory can still provoke an angry reaction. Messy demonstrates the lingering power of a carelessly weaponised word.

Crush

This is one of those words that has collected multiple meanings. We have the French to thank for this one – the original meaning was to smash or break; much later it came to mean humiliate or overpower. The word had no connection with infatuation until the expression 'to have a crush on' emerged in the early 20th century. And that's the type of crush that played a part in my story, as I'm sure it did (and still does) for millions of other teenage girls.

My first crush was on Davy Jones of The Monkees – the original manufactured boy band, assembled for an American TV series. He was cute, British and on my TV screen. The Monkees were the first band I ever saw play live, in 1967. My sister took me to see them at the Wembley Empire Pool in London. Even before support act Lulu appeared on stage I'd started hyperventilating and became so hysterical that I had to be taken out into a corridor by the nice man from St John's Ambulance. I recovered sufficiently to watch The Monkees play but they might as well have been miming. All I could hear was a cacophony of high-pitched screams (including my own).

Later, I went through a prog rock phase and my crush was Ted Turner, one of the guitarists in a band called Wishbone Ash. Then I moved on to Rod Stewart and the Faces before graduating to my first crush on a boy. He vaguely knew my sister and DJed at her 21st birthday party. I was an impressionable teen who'd never had a boyfriend; he was older and good looking. I spent a lot of time lurking around the turntables. It was excruciatingly obvious to everyone that I had a crush on him. And when he gave me a copy of David Bowie's album *Aladdin Sane*, I felt so special. In reality, he probably felt sorry for me. He was a disc jockey – he had plenty of copies of the album. He was never going to ask me out but it didn't stop me fantasising. It was an emotional pathway I wish, in hindsight, had never been created. Indeed, I would go on to experience the word even more fully as I was metaphorically crushed as a result of being attracted to unavailable or unsuitable men.

Postscript: Many years later, I met my childhood crush Davy Jones in unusual and slightly awkward circumstances. They say don't meet your heroes and they're right.

Stroke

Like the One Ring in *The Lord of the Rings* (my favourite book and movie trilogy of all time), in my story stroke is the One Word ThatRules Them All. In fact, I found myself looking at the word on this page and distracting myself – making a cup of tea, eating a biscuit, listening to a podcast – rather than sitting down to write about why this word has had such a profound impact on my life.

So, let's start at the beginning. It was April Fools' Day, 1973 – a couple of months before I sat my O-Levels. I was doing my homework in the lounge of our terraced house in Beckenham, Kent. Donny Osmond's 'Puppy Love' was playing on the radio, my younger brother was in the dining room watching *Thunderbirds*, my mum was preparing a roast chicken lunch in the kitchen and my dad was upstairs in the bathroom.

For some reason, my sister was at work. This was the only unusual thing about that quiet Sunday morning – that is, until I heard my dad stumbling down the stairs and into the lounge. I saw that his flies were undone and his trousers were gaping open. My first reaction was complete and utter embarrassment. Why on earth hadn't he zipped up? Shame was quickly replaced by panic when my mum followed him into the room shouting at me.

'Call the doctor!'

'What? Why?'

'Your father is having a stroke.'

'What's a stroke?'

'Never mind, I just know he's having a stroke and you need to call the doctor.'

'But I've never phoned the doctor before…'

'Just look up the number in the phone book in the hall.'

I didn't like making phone calls at the best of times. And this definitely wasn't the best of times. But the urgency in Mum's voice made me realise I had to get on with it and dial. I had no idea what a stroke was but by this point I'd figured out that it must be serious. It was, of course, a Sunday and the surgery was closed. I had to call the emergency number. I told a man that my dad was having a stroke and he said he'd send a locum. I didn't know what a locum was either but I told my mum one of them was coming.

The wait was interminable. The locum eventually arrived, examined my dad and told us to call an ambulance. Another interminable wait ensued. When the ambulance arrived, the paramedics strapped my dad into a weird seat/stretcher and wheeled him outside to the waiting vehicle.

My mum was right – my dad had just had a stroke.

It would take months, if not years, for me to understand exactly what that meant for him and for us. They called it a 'catastrophic stroke', which left him partially paralysed down one side of his body. The visible physical impairment was difficult enough to deal with but the invisible damage it wreaked on his brain was much harder to handle. He wasn't really capable of being my dad after that. The sunshine that had filled my childhood dimmed on that day.

I don't want to continue with this story. Even though I've told it many times before, in different ways, I'd still say that it's a life-defining story. That story made me grow up – quickly. It made me realise I couldn't depend on my family for financial support. It set me on a path to valuing self-sufficiency and independence more than anything else.

No one offered us any support or advice. We were left to our own devices to figure out how to care for Dad and adjust to the dramatic shift in family dynamics. I still believe that the aftermath of his stroke undermined my ability to form lasting relationships with men. It made me think that anyone I loved could be emotionally and psychologically ripped away from me in an instant. That's a heavy burden for one word to carry.

Stroke – so short yet so dynamic, with so many meanings. And so ironic that one of those meanings is so gentle, so soothing; and another refers to the action of a pen. Yet in my life, it has been a cutting, brutal and devastating word. And if God really did deliver it (the original meaning of the word was 'the stroke of God's hand'), God and I need to have a few words.

Pause for reflection

There are many definitions of the storytelling concept known as the 'inciting incident' but my favourite is this one, courtesy of Story Grid (2023): 'The inciting incident is a ball of chaos that spins into the story and knocks the protagonist's life out of balance.' That's a pretty accurate description of what happened to me on 1 April 1973. It was the pivotal moment when everything changed and there was no going back to the way things were. When you're drafting a book or keynote speech, the inciting incident provides a rich seam of life experience to dig into. Yours might not be as sudden as mine (and may have happened much earlier in life – even before you were born) but I'll bet you can identify one without too much trouble.

I'm reminded of Cariad Lloyd, host of the popular podcast *Griefcast*, writing in her book *You Are Not Alone* (2023) that she divides her life into 'before Dad died' (which happened when she was 15) and 'after Dad died'. This perfectly illustrates the ball of chaos that can blow up your life. You may, of course, have experienced more than one inciting incident in your life, or two in close proximity.

Can you trace a dotted line between an inciting incident in your life and where you are now? How has it impacted you? My dad's stroke severely affected his ability to communicate. I can make the case for this being one reason why I'm passionate about clarity of communication and creative self-expression and have been ever since I wrote my first article for publication – and maybe even before that. I'm only realising this as I'm writing, 50 years after my inciting incident. It's the gift that keeps on giving.

Sing

After writing about the One Word, it comes as a relief to reach the sunlit uplands of sing. And it's true to say that my ability to sing and enjoy singing carried me through the years following my dad's stroke. I've been able to carry a tune from an early age. I remember entertaining my Aunty Sheila and Uncle Trevor with a cheery rendition of 'Noisy Little Puffer Train' when I was only two and later bagging the lead role in my primary school's operetta. I loved the attention that singing brought me and the permission it gave shy (sorry, introverted) little me to take centre stage and occupy the spotlight.

So, when a group of friends – including my first proper boyfriend, Pete – decided to form a band in the late 1970s, I jumped at the chance to join them as a backing vocalist. It had started in the delightfully shambolic way in which many amateur combos come together – just a bunch of us messing around in someone's bedroom with a few guitars, a cheap keyboard (in my case a brown plastic organ from Woolworths, given to me as a surprise present by my parents one Christmas), plus bongos, maracas and whatever we could find in the kitchen to use as percussion. The band was more like a ramshackle theatre troupe – the only naturally talented musician was lead guitarist Colin. Rhythm guitarists Ken and John could play quite well and write a decent song but the rest of us just hit things and made noises.

We went on to become a moderately successful semi-pro pub rock band called Tennis Shoes. I loved singing – partly because I was able to release pent-up energy and partly because I could become someone else on stage (that would become an emerging theme), not that 'shy' girl and not the daughter who always felt sad about her father. We created our own form of gibberish – which was just as well because by this time there was a no-nonsense atmosphere and much less laughter at home.

Postscript: Forty years after quitting Tennis Shoes, I joined another band (The Subtle Genes) on backing vocals (and occasional lead vocals). I loved getting back on stage behind a microphone to live out my Debbie Harry fantasy once again.

Perform

This entry could easily have been performance or performer but I eventually landed on perform. As I mentioned in my reflections on the previous word, my ability to perform was noticed at an early age. I don't know if I wanted to perform at that time but I didn't complain about being trundled out for other people's entertainment. The desire to perform probably came later, when I played increasingly important roles in school stage shows, culminating in the lead role in the obscure operetta *Pearl the Fishermaiden*. I remember knowing the role was mine by rights. I was the best singer, the most popular girl, the most deserving of the top spot. I rarely experienced that level of confidence and certainty again.

However, it was during my participation in a strange suburban May Queen pageant that I started to make the connection between dressing up/playing a character and feeling attractive. I joined when I was nine or ten and worked my way up through the ranks (from attendant to page, crown bearer and prince), finally becoming Eden Park's May Queen at the age of 12, on the verge of puberty. There I was, once more the centre of attention, playing a role in costume. I danced around a maypole in a sparkly white and silver dress and tiara and had no idea that what I was doing was part of an ancient fertility ritual.

Later on, when I started performing with Tennis Shoes in the pubs of north London, my wardrobe evolved to include a series of increasingly scanty outfits. Again, I was the centre of attention; again, playing a role; again, in costume. Those were the conditions under which I allowed myself to 'show off'. It might seem counterintuitive for an introvert to enjoy performing in front of an audience but what made it acceptable was the permission to be in the spotlight and actively role-play. When I was on stage, I felt untouchable. Well, apart from the gig when Richard Branson (co-founder of Virgin Records) and Mike Oldfield (of *Tubular Bells* fame) tried to grab my ankles while dressed as adult babies in bonnets and nappies, but that's a story for another book.

Performing was a much-needed escape from the reality of life with a father who became the centre of attention for a different, unwanted reason. Along with domestic duties, I had to perform the role of dutiful daughter. I was good at that too, even though I resented it at times.

Belch

Perhaps I'm a prude but I don't like words that describe bodily functions. Belch is not my least favourite but I didn't want to choose fart because I despise that word (I prefer the gentler northern variation – trump, presumably from trumpet, as in, 'Have you just trumped?'). Like fart, belch is an Old English word; it originally meant 'poor beer'.

My enforced encounter with the word belch came

courtesy of a song. It was a malicious act by my boyfriend Pete, Tennis Shoes' keyboard player, to write lyrics featuring the words belch and fart and make me sing them. He knew it would make me feel uncomfortable. That was the level of his humour: let's see if we can make her squirm! The song he wrote, on which I sang lead vocals, was called 'Rolf Is Stranger Than Richard'. It was based on the 'hilarious' idea that the once popular (and now deceased) Australian entertainer Rolf Harris and equally popular (and also deceased) British actor Richard Harris were brothers – and that Rolf was 'the perfect man for me in every single way'. (The irony is not lost on me, given what subsequently emerged about Rolf – but in those days he was still a national treasure.) It gently lampooned him, playing to the stereotype that all Aussie men are oafs who belch and fart all day. The offending line was: 'And I still think of Australia when I hear you belch and f-a-a-a-a-a-a-a-a-art.' I hated singing it, especially because the 'fart' was so drawn out. I did not, and still do not, condone this kind of schoolboy joke. Get away from me with your unpleasant words.

Postscript: The offending (and offensive) song was chosen to appear on the B-side of the only single (that was, in fact, an EP) Tennis Shoes ever released. You can still hear it on the Tennis Shoes website. (Yes, there is a Tennis Shoes website – see the Resources section at the end of the book.) Quite improbably, a cutting from music magazine Sounds *posted on Twitter in 2022 resulted in the TV critic of the* Liverpool Echo *revealing that he still has a copy of the Tennis Shoes EP and that 'Rolf Is Stranger Than Richard' is his favourite track. You couldn't make it up.*

Single (Version 1)

Single – so close to sing, yet so far away. And yet, I did end up singing on a single (ie the Tennis Shoes EP). Singles – as in vinyl records played at 45 rpm – were an integral part of my teenage life. The first one I ever bought with my own money was 'No Matter What' by Badfinger (a hit in 1970). I felt so cool buying it because it was released on The Beatles' Apple label. After that, I developed a small yet eclectic singles collection that also (randomly) included the England World Cup Squad single, 'Back Home'. It had a strange B-side called 'Cinnamon Stick', which featured some particularly inane and nonsensical lyrics. B-sides were so often afterthoughts or songs that would never see the light of day anywhere else (ie not on an album). Like 'Cinnamon Stick', they became curiosities – until the double A-side came along.

As a family, we tuned in to the singles chart. Every Sunday afternoon, we'd gather over tea, sandwiches and tinned mandarin segments (with evaporated milk) to listen to the chart rundown on Radio 1. The announcement of the number one single often turned into a peak experience for me – particularly if I had an emotional investment in the artist. Two such moments occurred when T Rex reached number one with 'Hot Love' (1971) and 10cc with 'I'm Not in Love' (1975). However, as I moved through my teens, buying singles began to feel childish. This was particularly true while I was going through my prog rock phase, which was all about albums – often double or triple albums – and therefore considered to be the more mature purchase. But the word single, in one of its other guises, would go on to make a regular appearance in my life.

Secretary

I remember careers advice lessons being deadly dull, irrelevant and boring. If, like me, you weren't filling out an UCCA (university application) form, the careers teacher lost interest. There seemed to be only three viable career paths for girls in the mid-1970s: teacher, nurse or secretary. After my dad had a stroke, it was imperative for me to become financially independent, so I decided to take a secretarial course with a view to earning a decent wage when I left school. In those days secretarial work was highly skilled and well paid. It required excellent shorthand and typing speeds as well as organisational, planning and people skills. The dictionary definition (a person employed to assist with correspondence, make appointments and carry out administrative tasks) undersells it somewhat. The origin of the word is in 'secret' – as a secretary you are the keeper of secrets, the trusted assistant.

Armed with my certificates for shorthand (top speed of 120 words per minute) and typing (60 words per minute), I secured my first secretarial job at the Department of the Environment in Westminster. My first boss was a kindly government scientist who was approaching retirement. He'd been involved in the design of the zebra crossing and Belisha beacon, which I thought was impressive. He became something of a father figure and introduced me to avocados (which, at the time, were terribly exotic). My next boss was also a government scientist, also approaching retirement, but he wasn't as cool as my first boss. He didn't seem to do much at all, so neither did I.

Then another, completely different, role beckoned: secretary to the editor of *Sounds*, one of the three major rock music weeklies of the late 1970s. I ended up quitting the establishment for the anti-establishment. One of my weekly tasks was to call our star columnist, the legendary Radio 1 DJ John Peel, to beg, cajole and wheedle some words out of him before the print deadline. At first, the thought of taking dictation from such a countercultural hero reduced me to jelly but we became firm phone friends and he kindly played the Tennis Shoes single several times on his late-night show.

As I became an integral part of the *Sounds* machine, Tennis Shoes benefited from a gig review. It was exhilarating to see the band's name – and my own – in print in a national music paper. 'Tennis Shoes can best be described as a comedy band with overt rock influences,' it read, 'but then they're also a show, a parody, a satire, an outrage and a spectacle.' I was singled out for praise for having a voice 'reminiscent of Little Eva', and decided to practise singing 'The Locomotion' to see if the writer was correct.

Even though it helped the band a little, in the end my role as secretary at *Sounds* helped me a great deal more. It was during this time that I wrote my first review and had it published. It was the first of many. I split up with the band's keyboard player and started a relationship with a much older *Sounds* journalist. I didn't want to sing about belching and farting any more, so I sacrificed my 'career' as a semi-pro performer and quit the band. Secretary fitted with Tennis Shoes and my teenage self but not with Ray-Bans and rock journalism.

Pause for reflection

In my own life dictionary, the series of words that emerged after 'stroke' tells the story of how I responded to my inciting incident. But how did you respond to yours? It might have happened earlier or later than mine but you'll know how it affected you and the decisions you subsequently made about your life and work. Again, this is fertile territory for you to explore as it will be foundational to the development of your character and personality.

I withdrew emotionally but also put myself out there – up on stage, performing. There's no doubt that I started to express myself but at the same time I needed the security of a sensible job. This was the start of a dynamic that would continue to play itself out.

Specificity is important in storytelling. For example, rather than saying 'I joined a band with a few friends', I wrote that it was 'a bunch of us messing around in someone's bedroom with a few guitars, a cheap keyboard (in my case a brown plastic organ from Woolworths, given to me as a surprise present by my parents one Christmas), plus bongos, maracas and whatever we could find in the kitchen to use as percussion.' That plastic organ is still vivid in my memory so it felt important to describe it in all its glory. This is also an example of a 'gleaming detail' that brings a story to life.

Here are some prompts to help you uncover the words that impacted you during your troubled (or perhaps untroubled) teens and as a result shed light on what might have been your inciting incident. Again, carve out time and a quiet space, choose one or two questions that speak to you and keep writing in a stream of conscious-ness for at least five minutes without stopping to read what you've written. You can always go back and develop the story later.

- *Which words did you hear in your teenage years that pierced your heart and soul?*
- *Which words encouraged and affirmed you?*
- *Which words linger in your memory that you didn't really understand at the time?*
- *Which words from this time in your life can still provoke a strong reaction?*
- *Which words stand out from your teenage diary?*
- *Which word connects you to your inciting incident?*

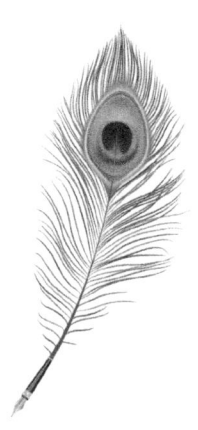

Chapter 4
Early adult words

As you mature, your vocabulary expands and evolves to reflect your emerging identity. At least, that's the hope. Some words will become bespoke labels you're proud to wear; others will become charity shop rejects that belong in the recycling bin. Some words will help you feel included, others excluded. But now you have agency, you get to choose the words that accompany you on your journey and define the story you tell about yourself.

A couple of the words I've picked in this chapter are *literally* adult words, which I could never have anticipated when I was a modest and self-effacing secretary by day and backing singer in a semi-professional band by night. After I entered the wild world of pop and rock music, it was perhaps inevitable that I'd experiment with mild acts of transgression. Maybe that word should be on this list – but underneath the costumes and behind the masks, I saw myself as a 'good girl' at heart.

I decided to name this section 'early adult words' to guide you towards the words that were (and still are) important influences from that stage of your life, which will probably prompt stories that relate to your professional life as much as your personal life.

Writer

I was able to take complete ownership of this word when I became a full-time staff writer on *Sounds* in the summer of 1980. This was my new identity. I could say 'I am a writer' – a totally different story to 'I am a secretary'. It transformed the way people perceived me and the way I perceived myself. Even though I'd been good at writing little essays at primary school, I didn't aspire to become a professional writer. It wasn't on the list of career options presented to me at school. But by the age of 23 I'd made the unlikely leap from typist of another man's memos to author of my own thoughts and opinions – a radically different and more creative use of the manual typewriter I'd been trained to strike. I could've chosen 'journalist' but writer is the word that resonates with me the most. A writer of stories and articles as an occupation – that kind of writer.

I was talent-spotted by my own boss – the late, lamented Alan Lewis, editor of *Sounds*. He encouraged and supported my development as a writer while I was still his secretary. As I grew in confidence, I developed a strong point of view, which was essential if you wanted to be a rock critic. And when the time came for *Sounds* to expand its staff, Alan offered me a staff writer's job. It was an extraordinary opportunity that I grabbed with both hands (and one pen). I was mesmerised by reading my words in print. It felt as if a new part of me had been born – a part that had never been seen or heard before. I could express myself fully in the written word and while my words were widely read, I could still hide behind them. I didn't need to make myself visible beyond the odd byline photo and that suited me.

As I embraced this exciting new identity as a writer, the

world opened up to me. I went from being confined to an office in London to travelling all over the world, interviewing bands and writing reviews and features. When I look back, it still seems unbelievable to me that I became a writer without any formal training or previous experience – but it happened. And I'm still, and always will be, a writer of articles.

Nom de plume

OK, let's back up here for a moment. I've trumpeted my arrival as a professional scribe and expressed amazement that my words could appear in print. But there's something you need to know. It wasn't me. Well, it was me – but I was hiding behind someone else's name. Why? Because, as previously mentioned, I'd been a secretary. And secretaries should know their place, right? And in those days, their place was behind a typewriter typing an important man's words and taking an important man's calls.

I was forced to use a pseudonym because the publishers of *Sounds* imagined that if I, a mere secretary, could make it into print, then hundreds of other secretaries would get ideas 'above their station' and want to become writers too. At least I imagine that's what they were afraid of. The other reason was that my first articles were published while I was on the payroll and the only way I could get paid for my freelance writing was to set up an account using a different name. So I had to find a suitable nom de plume (so much more interesting and colourful than the pedestrian 'pen name'). Despite the fact that so many of our words are French in origin, the irony is that nom de plume is a faux French phrase coined by an obscure Victorian novelist. How funny that nom de plume itself is fake!

This, then, is the story of how I found my nom de plume. It was my then boyfriend Tony Mitchell, fellow *Sounds* writer, who suggested the name Betty Page. Back in 1979, only committed fans of underground publications knew the name Betty Page (although the woman herself actually used the spelling Bettie). In the 1950s, she had been a counter-cultural heroine, the 'anti-Marilyn Monroe', if you like. By day she was a pin-up model in leopard-skin swimsuits who posed for covers of cheesy compilation albums but by night she modelled for thousands of mildly titillating photographs depicting her nude or in her scanties and stilettos, often tied up with rope or brandishing a riding crop over a supine woman. She was covertly worshipped by men the world over and Tony in particular. There was something mischievous about using the name of a real person who was well known in certain circles but unknown to the general public. To the select few, her name was like a secret code. And it fitted so well: like my own, the first name began with B; the second was a nod to appearing in print. It was the perfect disguise.

The weird part is that Bettie disappeared from public view around the time I was born, only to reappear in the late 1980s – after I'd stopped using her name. She went on to become a more mainstream cultural figure and had a film made about her life (*The Notorious Bettie Page*, 2006). I'm extremely grateful to her for lending me (a version of) her name. As a tribute, I have an original photo of her on my wall in which she's wearing a leopard-skin swimsuit and dangling from a branch with a knife between her teeth. It inspires me to be bold, brave and fierce!

New Romantic

It was my first major achievement as a staff writer on *Sounds*: not only securing an interview with Spandau Ballet, who were the coolest band in London at the dawn of a new decade, but also enshrining in print a term that would launch a youth movement and become part of the pop culture lexicon. Over the years there has been considerable debate about exactly who coined the term New Romantic (and its plural, New Romantics). I'm sure I'd heard it used to describe the Blitz Kids (the group of colourfully dressed young people who frequented the Blitz nightclub in London's Covent Garden in 1979–80) but in those heady pre-internet days when social media was beyond anyone's imagination, a cultural phenomenon only came into being if it had appeared in the pages of a magazine or newspaper. And the moment that this particular phenomenon was recorded for posterity was in September 1980, when the headline on my interview with Spandau Ballet in *Sounds* read: 'The New Romantics – a Manifesto for the 80s'.

I can't remember if the headline was my idea or Alan's (he later assured me it was mine) but it's universally acknowledged to be the first mention in print of what would go on to represent an entire genre of music. Many years later, Spandau Ballet's Gary Kemp told me that he'd given a framed copy of the centre-spread *Sounds* interview to his eldest son, Finlay, to show him where it all began. He would also credit me in his autobiography with coining the term – and that's as close to an official blessing as you can get. This is how he explained the meaning of the term New Romantic in his book *I Know This Much: From Soho to Spandau* (2009): 'Betty's title seemed to sum up the anachronism of the fashions and the whimsical approach to clothes to the mood-noise of the lyrics and music, with its conceit that it all meant something grander; and – above all – because of the name's association with the original Romantics, Byron and Shelley – it highlighted the cult of self, a powerful philosophy that would exemplify the coming decade.'

There I was, a baby writer with a nom de plume, already having an influence on the English language. Not bad, as far as claims to fame go. But was I a New Romantic myself? Hmmm… I tried, but not really. I was an interested observer who wore frilly shirts from Top Shop (not so cool).

Spesh

Introducing the term New Romantic(s) to British lexicographers wasn't the end of my influence on the English language. Several years later, I received an email from a researcher who worked for the *Oxford English Dictionary*. His editor had asked him to check a quotation from a review I'd written about the B-52s' *Mesopotamia* album in *Sounds* in 1982. The line that attracted his editor's attention was: 'Since this is more like an extended dub 12-inch dancefloor spesh than your actual elpee, what's truly noo in the groove is precious.' He was interested in the usage of 'spesh', asking for verification and hopefully a reference copy of the original print edition (which I no longer had).

Well, spesh was simply my way of abbreviating special, a word that doesn't really need to be abbreviated, and it surprised me that it might end up in an edition of the *OED*. He didn't seem interested in my use of elpee (long-playing record, obviously) or noo (new), just spesh – which I doubt is used in that context by anybody any more. As someone who's constantly alarmed by the way in which text speak and emojis have undermined the English language, I now realise that I may have been responsible for part of this dumbing-down process. I hang my head in shame. I have googled spesh (a word that dates back to Victorian times) and am even more alarmed to learn that in current slang it means 'retard'. But that's the thing about language: it evolves and you can't stop the evolution. You could say my casual use of this made-up word to connect with the readers of *Sounds* (ie me getting down with the kids) was the thumbs-up or winky emoji of its day.

Pop

I could've included rock on this list (I did, after all, pride myself on being known as a rock journalist when I started out) but pop trumped it in the end. Why? Because I grew up with pop music as pop music itself was growing up. The word first appeared a few years before I was born to describe a modern style of popular youth music that went on to take over the world. I succumbed to Beatlemania as it was happening and became a superfan of the world's first TV-generated pop group, The Monkees. Even during the prog rock phase of my teens, my love of pop music still lurked in the background. In fact, when I was hired by *Sounds*, I'm convinced it was because they wanted a woman to write about pop music (which was considered to be girly and fluffy) so that the blokes could focus on covering the 'serious' rock bands like The Clash and The Jam.

It so happened that the music emerging in the early 1980s – much of which was dependent on the affordable new electronic technology being imported from Japan – suited the pop label. And many of the bands I interviewed and championed – Spandau Ballet, Duran Duran, Depeche Mode, Soft Cell, The Human League, to name a few – would shortly take the charts by storm on both sides of the Atlantic.

I never thought there was a stigma attached to being a pop as opposed to a rock group. After all, if your music is popular, you must be doing something right… right? I've never bought into the snobbery of musical purism, of only appealing to a niche audience. I was a popular girl at primary school who turned into a popular pop writer. I wouldn't be surprised if pop made it onto your list, too – in its social or musical context. Small word, lasting effect.

Gossip

The Old English version of this word actually meant godparent but went on to mean women exchanging chit-chat while attending a birth and later anyone engaging in idle talk. I can see the misogyny here, as it infers that only women gossip. Now, I would *not* like my friends and family to think of me as a gossip but, for a few years, I was a gossip columnist (for the pop magazines *Noise!* and *Record Mirror*) – not a tabloid newspaper type of gossip columnist (they were ruthless) but more of an observer of pop stars and their shenanigans. I was adept at spotting faces and remembering names – useful skills when you're at a record company party, a nightclub or mingling backstage at a gig.

I was also an accomplished wallflower, able to disappear into the background whenever necessary – another useful skill to have when famous people were misbehaving in front of me. I never knowingly said anything malicious about anyone or invented anything about them. It was all relatively good natured but I had full permission to take the mickey out of pop stars. I loved being 'in the know' and pop stars knowing that I was going to write about them. I was good at picking up undercurrents and what was really going on between people. So, for me, gossip remains a positive word. It connected me with people I admired, people who made me laugh and people with whom I socialised.

There's a photograph that was taken of me with my then best friend Gill Smith at London's Limelight nightclub in the 1980s. We're both wearing glamorous vintage frocks and holding glasses of (free) champagne. We exude a Hedda Hopper and Louella Parsons vibe (the two glamazons of gossip during the Golden Age of Hollywood), which seems appropriate, as we were both gossip columnists at the time.

These days I'm extremely mindful about gossip. I understand that telling tales and sharing rumours behind people's backs is not healthy behaviour. But I'll always acknowledge the light-heartedness and fun that writing a gossip column brought into my life. As far as I'm aware, in this innocent world, years before social media and trolling, no one was harmed on my watch.

In a programme broadcast in August 2022, BBC Radio 4's *Woman's Hour* explored the topic of women and gossip. In an accompanying article, Professor Melanie Tebbutt from Manchester Metropolitan University stated that throughout history, gossip has been a way for women to take up space: 'It was a space from which men were excluded. Men were extremely curious as to what went on there and what they were talking about… But there was this sense that women were occupying a space through their speech, which was separate.' This all puts gossip in a much more empowering frame and is in the spirit of how I experienced it myself.

Pause for reflection

This is the 'rising action' sequence of my life dictionary or, as Story Grid describes it, the 'progressive complications' stage, as the protagonist (me) tries to restore the balance that was knocked off kilter by the inciting incident. This is where the stakes are progressively raised. I became a professional writer (yippee, who'd have thought?) and had an immediate impact on popular culture and language. That's me expressing myself right there. All good, right? Yes and no. I'd been thrust into a place of high visibility where my words really counted, thanks to my first two mentors, Tony and Alan – people who believed in me before I believed in myself. They opened doors for me that I didn't know existed. But complications were bubbling under the surface. I had a pen name to hide behind and a reputation to live up to. I was excited but easily overwhelmed. And I hadn't begun to acknowledge or process what had happened to my dad.

Do you resonate with this? What were/are your progressive complications as they relate to your inciting incident? What problems were/are you grappling with at the heart of your story? And who were/are your mentors? Take your time to reflect on these words and the stories they evoke – it will be worth its weight in gold.

Stilettos

I often wonder whether I became obsessed with stilettos in my twenties because my mum wouldn't let me wear kitten heels in my early teens. When I was finally able to make my own footwear purchasing decisions, I went through a platforms phase before buying my first serious pair of high heels in the late 1970s – a pair of snub-nosed, bright red 1950s-style patent leather stilettos with a four-inch heel, originally made for Malcolm McLaren and Vivienne Westwood's King's Road boutique, Sex. These were exactly the type of shoes that my namesake Bettie Page used to wear in her glamour shots. These shoes rocked – and rolled my ankles. I got attention in these shoes. I rocked. Then I became a rock journalist – one who vowed never to wear boring, flat shoes.

As I climbed the career ladder, I tottered on towers of power and my enraptured boyfriend Tony reminded me that skyscraper stilettos – the heels of which could reach the giddy height of six inches – give you a swagger, an assertive strut. Dizzying heels required a power wardrobe: tailored suits, pencil skirts, seamed stockings. I felt as if my time had come when, in the early 1980s, fashion, music and self-expression came together in a burst of colour and style – and I embraced it wholeheartedly. Whether I was wearing a second-hand cocktail dress, a vintage 1920s flapper jacket or a daringly short miniskirt (which Boy George told me he thoroughly disapproved of), high heels were the perfect accessories.

I became obsessed with shiny red stilettos and graduated to a dayglo scarlet pair with slim, vertiginous heels. I wore these with immense pride, matching them with a super-short red and black pleated satin skirt and unusual hosiery with one red leg and one black leg. Proper stilettos – anything from three inches upwards – made you stand on the balls of your feet, accentuating your calves and your curves. In short, they made you look, and feel, sexy. This was new and exciting to me in my rock journalist era.

The fact that I was prepared to suffer the discomfort of wearing high heels in order to feel more empowered says a lot about what it was like to be a young woman in the 1980s. But the higher the heel, the further the fall. I was projecting an image of power when what I felt inside was… powerless.

Fetish

It's strange to think of it now but this word became part of my everyday vocabulary for many years. It first emerged in the 17th century to denote an object worshipped for its magical powers. I find this amusing, given the nature of my introduction to fetishism.

It was on a trip to Manhattan in 1981 to interview the electronic pop duo Soft Cell that I encountered my first shoe fetishist, who was so taken with my high heels and delicate feet (size 4) that he asked me to stand on the draining board of the kitchen at the nightclub Danceteria so that he could take photographs of me from the waist down. And so it was that I embarked on several adventures foot first, enjoying my impact on the male imagination. Pointed symbols of feminine power required a step into a different world, one in which women dressed in leather and latex and assumed a position of dominance.

During my brief stint as a fetish model, my crowning moment arrived when I was invited to pose (in exquisite agony) in a pair of seamed black stockings and six-inch black patent heels for the cover of the fetish magazine *Skin Two*, an image that went on to inspire many copycats and provided fantasies for generations of foot fetishists. But the photo, arresting though it was, focused on the shoe and a small portion of my ankle and calf – an objectification that had little to do with who I really was. I was just playing at being Miss Whiplash. I may have looked like a dominatrix (see the next entry) but inside I was still a girl who was playing dress-up.

Fetish gave me access to an underground movement. I'd never felt embraced by the New Romantic crowd but I was a major player in London's nascent fetish club scene. When Skin Two, the nightclub, opened in 1983, my membership card sported the number 001. Queen of the 1980s fetish scene, that was me. Or was it Betty? Looking back and now knowing the origin of the word, I can appreciate its association with sorcery. The heels, the wig, the latex wardrobe – it was all witchcraft; I was actively weaving a spell.

Dominatrix

I was reluctant to include this word but a few of my friends argued that it was essential. It seems that, even though I was never a real-life dominatrix, at times I've exuded the air of a 'dominant female entity'. As the previous entry attests, I enjoyed dressing up in the attire of a dominatrix but the idea of being a practising 'dom' didn't interest me at all. Well, that's not quite true. When I was in New York with Soft Cell, I met the apprentice of a notorious dominatrix called Angel Stern who almost convinced me to become one of Angel's apprentices. I confess to being tempted at the time but ultimately declined the invitation.

Appearing to be confident and in complete control provided the perfect way to conceal how I was feeling inside. Dressing in this way made me look scary and unapproachable, which protected my sensitive inner core. No one was going to mess with a woman who regularly carried a riding crop. I was playing a role – one that, to start with, I enjoyed. It was really a form of drag – dressing up to express a side of my personality that only emerged in costume and with a lot of make-up.

But this role-playing eventually started to become a drag of a different kind. On one dark day in the early 1990s, I packed a suitcase full of my prized footwear and latex outfits and placed it next to the bins. It broke my heart to abandon the costumes that had defined my image for so long but my sense of self was at stake. It was a symbolic act, putting it all out with the rubbish so I could start afresh. I didn't sell any of it because I couldn't face anyone else wearing my disguise.

These days, I don't need a costume. I'd like to think I'm a dominant female entity in my own right – stiletto heels and riding crop not required. In fact, I was stunned when a colleague of mine used the word dominatrix to describe me. She knew nothing of my story. So, it seems that, even without the outer layer, the word dominatrix really did get under my skin and stayed there. I'm still surprisingly good at cracking the whip when I need to – but not for anyone's pleasure.

Pause for reflection

You may be surprised by this particular run of progressive complications. There's plenty of evidence that I might have taken 'self-expression by any means necessary' a little too far but I can see how it related to my inciting incident. The bold outer appearance masked an inner fragility that I didn't want anyone to see.

Your progressive complications might be challenges or conflicts you faced/are facing as a result of your response to your inciting incident. They might be successes followed by failures, or vice versa. Whatever yours might be, they will certainly have tested your resources. You probably won't

Early adult words

have faced them on your own, though, as you'll often have encountered/are encountering real-life 'magical helpers' who arrive at just the right moment (and often only briefly) to encourage and support you.

The words you unearth here may guide you to stories of triumph over adversity or tests of faith, resilience and endurance. Which words forged you in life's fire? Which words provided you with tough life lessons?

Single (Version 2)

The first singles I ever (favourably) reviewed as a music journalist were 'Happy House' by Siouxsie and the Banshees and 'Baggy Trousers' by Madness, both released in 1980. Reviewing the singles was a prestigious gig at a weekly music paper. You were able to be *the* tastemaker and trendsetter. Singles were the bread and butter of all pop magazines. Whatever made the charts made it into those pages.

I loved singles. But I didn't want to be single. I hated being single.

After experiencing an emotional car crash of conflicting identities and transgressive experimentation, my first long-term adult relationship ended and left me wandering naked on the highway, so to speak. Despite my latex armour, I felt exquisitely exposed as a woman who 'dressed for sex' (yes, that's how it was judged at the time) in an industry full of men looking for instant gratification. I realised how protected I'd felt by being in a relationship. Now I was on my own.

I was saved, in a sense, by my close friendship with the aforementioned Gill Smith, who in many ways was every bit as lost as I was. She worked as a PR for a record company and we met when I went to interview one of her bands. When my relationship ended, she took me in, and we began our adventures – two single women who called themselves the 'Rubber Goddesses'. Together, dressed in latex and stilettos by night, we created our own fortress: impenetrable and unassailable.

One of our favourite singles was 'You Spin Me Round (Like A Record)' by Dead or Alive. That was our 'getting ready to go out' music. It always put us in the mood. I loved going out with Gill – there was never a dull moment. Both of us were propelled into a few ill-advised liaisons with unsuitable men. But my suitable woman was always there for me – at least until I met a suitable man.

Astrology

My fascination with astrology began in 1979 when a friend gifted me a little book about my sun sign, Aquarius. I soon realised that magazine and newspaper horoscopes only scratched the surface and became a voracious reader of astrology books, learning the symbolic language of astrology and painstakingly calculating and drawing my birth chart by hand. The predictive aspects of astrology didn't interest me as much – it was more about the light it could shed on my personality and what motivated me to behave in particular ways. Was it nature or nurture? I remember the moment I discovered that my birth chart featured a relatively rare and challenging aspect pattern known as a grand cross, consisting of four planets in square to each other (separated by 90 degrees) and two pairs of planets in opposition. Aha, I thought – this is why I suffer! For I am always at cross purposes with myself!

I allowed myself to feel like a planetary victim, weighed

down by this cross. I interpreted the tension inherent in my birth chart as the reason why I lived a double life (Beverley and Betty) – a split personality pulling in opposite directions. It was extraordinary to me how accurately my chart described the two extremes of my character – the sensitive, spiritual, introverted side and the risk-taking, taboo-busting, exhibitionist side. Every time the dominatrix asserted herself, it would hurt the reserved people-pleaser; and every time the sensitive introvert took hold, the dominatrix either rejected her or harmed her in some way.

Much later, I discovered a more nuanced meaning. Oriented in one's inner world, the grand cross often signifies stubbornness and resistance to change. On the positive side, it brings stability and strong willpower – and I've certainly been known to dig my heels in. It also greatly affects self-worth, causing either a profound sense of self-doubt or an inherent feeling of distinctiveness. Again, I've experienced both – but mostly self-doubt, even in the face of personal achievement.

However, I must add that this aspect pattern is only part of the bigger picture painted by my birth chart, which has provided me with a powerful map to guide me through life and support me through challenging times. It has also helped me to make sense of events that were beyond my control. I've studied astrology at Oxford University's summer schools and have a bookcase full of volumes on the subject. I still find that understanding the planetary weather helps me navigate the way forward. Whether or not it makes any logical or scientific sense, astrology speaks the language of my soul.

The original meaning of the word is 'study of the stars', although astrology is really about the planets in our solar system. I prefer to think of it as a search for meaning in the sky – 'as above, so below'. I still love gazing at the night sky on a clear night, in awe at the majesty of our solar system and universe. I feel connected to the planets in an instinctive, illogical way and always will.

Therapy

After acquiring a nom de plume and effectively splitting my personality, the therapist's couch became my inevitable destination. The more I played with the Betty Page image, the one I projected to the world in the pages of a pop magazine and the fetish clubs of London, the less happy and confident Beverley became. I started to believe I was only interesting and attractive as Betty, that the real me underneath the layers of disguise just wasn't enough. She was still the sad girl with a disabled dad mourning the loss of a father figure. Things got worse after I split up with my boyfriend, Tony, and my emotional stability went out of the window.

At some point in the mid-1980s, I ended up sitting in a courtyard in Covent Garden, feeling completely overwhelmed and about to start my first therapy session. Over the course of approximately 20 years, I would go on to see a variety of therapists and counsellors as I tried to find the underlying cause of my emotional and psychological issues, wrestling with the contradictions within my personality and my seeming inability to feel emotionally fulfilled.

I'd never dismiss the value of talk therapy but I eventually stopped looking for answers in the therapist's chair. I realised that therapy had given me an intellectual understanding of my problems but hadn't helped me to change my behaviour. My mum always used to say that therapy was 'navel gazing' but one thing it did do was help me to know myself on a deeper level. I was never ashamed to say I was in therapy, so it's a word I'm fully prepared to celebrate. The roots of the word lead to Ancient Greece and its original meaning – healing. And that's the one that I feel most connected to – *therapeía*.

The language around mental health is so much more sophisticated these days – and the support is on the whole easier to access (if you have the money). I spent a lot of time and money trying to 'fix' myself when what I really needed was to love myself, flaws and all, and process my suppressed emotions.

Editor

The professional climb that began with writer reached a base camp marked editor. In hindsight, I preferred the idea of being an editor over the reality of it. I became the editor of a pop magazine called *Record Mirror* in 1987 but – perhaps surprisingly, given that I embraced the image of the dominatrix – I didn't enjoy being in charge, even though I often referred to myself as the 'editrix'. I loved being part of a team but as soon as I became boss, the team's attitudes changed. Everyone who had unresolved issues with authority seemed to project them onto me. While I enjoyed telling people I was the editor, I found the experience isolating. I wasn't good at delegating or asking for help, so in many ways it was a recipe for disaster. After a few months, my deputy resigned because I didn't give him enough to do (sorry, Jim). I tried to run the magazine by committee, attempting to find a consensus about everything. When that didn't work, I went to the opposite extreme and dictated what was going in it.

After less than two years on the job and despite the fact

that I was in therapy, I hit burnout. I resigned, believing myself to be an abject failure. I was shocked and touched when I read the messages from the staff in my leaving card. They had valued and respected me so much more than I had valued and respected myself.

Since then, I have been a commissioning editor, a production editor, a sub-editor and a developmental editor. All important roles but not the top job. Sadly, my experience of editorship resulted in a lack of belief in my leadership abilities, which took years to overcome. I also fell into the trap of editing myself – only showing others what I wanted to show, never the full picture. I'm not saying I'm showing the full picture now, as writing about my chosen words is still a selective process, but I am revealing more of myself than I have before – and you may find the same when you're compiling your life dictionary.

I've now reclaimed the word and still describe myself, among other things, as an editor with a particularly good eye for detail and a passion for precision and clarity. The origin of the word is in the Latin *editor*, meaning 'one who puts forth'. And I've definitely done my fair share of putting forth.

Pause for reflection

Having completed this chapter, I can see that I paid a price for my response to the inciting incident and the progressive complications became… well, progressively damaging to my core self, despite my professional achievements. I appeared to be successful but didn't feel like a success because I valued emotional fulfilment (which I lacked) more than money and status (which I had, to a degree). Reaching burnout was my first crisis point. According to Story Grid, 'The crisis is what forces the protagonist to change and reveals their true character.' For me, it led to a complete re-evaluation of my priorities. My fear was that I'd become so stressed that I might have a stroke like my dad.

Have you tried to juggle a similar dilemma in your life? Have you experienced tension between your personal and professional selves? If you can tease out this story (or stories) through the gateway of your key words you'll find so much wisdom and insight that can add immense value to your thought leadership and storytelling.

What story do your 'early adult words' tell about you? The prompts below are here to guide you. As before, give yourself dedicated time and space to do this exercise without distractions. Pick as many questions as you want to answer. Grab your notebook and pen and keep writing until you run out of things to share. Don't worry if what you've written doesn't seem to make sense yet – this is the chance for your unconscious mind to deliver up hidden goodies.

- Which words were/are a good fit for you in early adulthood?
- Which words would you like to discard?
- Which words made/make you feel proud?

In Your Own Words

- ✍ *Which words are key to your 'progressive complications'?*
- ✍ *Which word triggers your crisis point?*
- ✍ *Who were/are your mentors and helpers?*
- ✍ *Which words inspire(d) you?*
- ✍ *Which words undermine(d) you?*

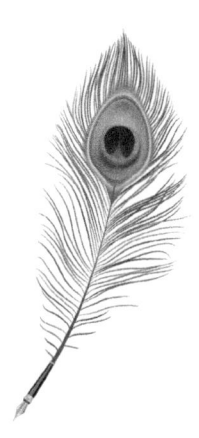

Chapter 5
Midlife words

In my experience, the funny thing about midlife is that you don't admit you've reached it until it's over and you're out the other side. Or perhaps it's easier to think of midlife as starting in your early forties and going on until you're in your seventies. Who knows? My mum used to talk about 'old people' in her nineties. Whatever your numerical age, you'll have your own perception of midlife and the words you associate with it.

After completing this chapter, I found that some of my words were easier to bear than others. Some of them elicited complex, nuanced stories that I can only touch on here; others led to black holes I'd rather avoid but must dive back into in order to make sense of them. As I continued writing, I felt heavier and heavier until it felt as if I was wading through wet concrete. I questioned whether I really wanted to write about these words – but persevered. Your experience might be easier than mine but this section of your life dictionary will probably feature a few weighty words. And if you haven't quite reached midlife, what would you *like* your midlife words to be?

Observer

This word symbolises one of my defining moments. I started my career in journalism as the proverbial fly on the wall, carefully observing everything that was going on around me. I often noticed things that others missed – relationships, asides, body language, the energy in the room – which enhanced my storytelling. It therefore seemed more than appropriate, after I had ended my career as a music journalist by clawing my way back from burnout with a glorious three-year stint at the *New Musical Express*, that I'd end up working for *The Observer*. Writing for a highbrow Sunday newspaper was an extraordinary and unexpected leap that marked what I think of as my peak career years. I was eventually appointed deputy editor of the newspaper's magazine supplement and was ambitious enough to have craved the top job. I didn't reach that position but treasured my time in the rarefied atmosphere of a venerable broadsheet and learned so much about my resilience and ability to bounce back.

Working for *The Observer* boosted my confidence and led to many years of rewarding jobs in what was known as Fleet Street (although by this time none of the newspapers were actually located there). It helped me to believe in myself again – as Beverley. I no longer required the nom de plume.

Observer is another old French word, of course. Apart from 'watch over, perceive, notice' it also meant seeing and noticing omens, good or bad. I'm good at seeing signs, noticing and then commenting on what I've noticed. I'm a natural observer. I believe that the world needs more thoughtful observers and fewer mindless participants.

Prelapsarian

I've included this as an example of a word I'd never use. Do you know what it means? Well, I certainly didn't when I first saw it in print. It featured in an article written for *The Observer* by the novelist Will Self, which I'd been tasked with editing. Mr Self is a writer who likes to dazzle with his intellect and vocabulary. But his use of a word like prelapsarian angered me. Good journalism is about effective communication and therefore using language that's clear and easy for readers to understand. I wanted to delete or change the word in Self's copy but was overruled because he was (and still is) a celebrated novelist.

Thanks to him, the word has stayed with me – but I always have to look up what it means and I've never used it in a sentence (written or spoken). To me, the word represents language that divides – you either get it or you don't. I don't. Perhaps I have a chip on my shoulder because I didn't go to university or study the classics but I don't use words to make myself look clever. I use words to convey meaning, to entertain and delight, to describe and evoke. If you, the reader, have to consult a dictionary to understand my writing, then I've failed. I believe in making the complex plain, not making the plain more complex. I agree with Stephen King, who wrote in 1986, 'Any word you have to hunt for in a thesaurus is the wrong word. There are no exceptions to this rule.' If you're interested, prelapsarian means innocent and unspoilt and relates to the time before the biblical Fall of Adam and Eve. So now you know, try using it in conversation. When choosing my language, I prefer to follow the advice of Bobette Buster in *Do Story*: 'Avoid multisyllabic, erudite, four-dollar words, over-intellectualising, philosophising, qualifying. See how many I just used? It's boring to keep reading them, isn't it?'

Invisible

They say that every action has an equal and opposite reaction and so it was that after my years of sartorial experimentation and exhibitionism, I became the invisible woman. Having disposed of my latex wardrobe and high heels, I started to dress in an inconspicuous way so that I could blend into the background even more. And after having been highly visible as a pop writer and editor, I was now, more often than not, tucked away at the back of a newspaper office. Having ditched Betty, on the rare occasion when I did have a story published, it would be under my real name and therefore few people knew of my legacy.

The work of a newspaper sub-editor (often abbreviated to 'sub') is highly skilled and requires an eye for detail as well as the ability to write a snappy headline. I've known many sub-editors over the years and admire them all. I think of them as invisible menders – skilfully patching up and improving stories so that no one, not even the writer, can see the joins. But, unlike the writers and reporters, they're rarely (if ever) credited in the newspaper. So, following my peak career years at *The Observer*, I spent years as an invisible mender, toiling away behind the scenes. I was content to stay in the shadows. I did, however, benefit from wearing the cloak of invisibility. I could switch into full observer mode, watching and noticing and making notes until someone noticed me.

Again, we can thank the French for this word: originally meaning 'incapable of being seen', it was only in the 1600s that it came to mean 'kept out of sight', which is exactly what I was doing. I didn't want to be seen; I wanted to hide. It took many years for me to want to become visible again.

Camaraderie

One of the best things about working in a newspaper office (as I did from the mid-1990s to the mid-2010s) was the camaraderie. There was something about the relentless deadlines that brought people together and produced a work hard/play hard culture. I'd enjoyed banter with colleagues at most of the magazines and music papers I'd worked for – *Sounds*, *Record Mirror*, *NME* – but newspapers were a different beast. That was down to the legacy of legendary Fleet Street characters and the stories told about them. These stories were recounted repeatedly, often embellished each time with an extra flourish for good measure. Most of these stories revolved around big personalities, alcohol and punch-ups. How any of these papers came out at all is astonishing given the amount of alcohol journalists consumed back in the day. It was par for the course to go drinking at lunchtime, come back to the office and be able to come up with brilliant headlines while completely blotto.

When I worked at the *Sunday Express* in the early 2000s, the editor of the *Daily Express* would take up residence at the local wine bar from about midday onwards. He bought a drink for anyone he knew and wouldn't take no for an answer. I'd often politely decline but would still find a bottle of Chardonnay waiting for me on the bar. He'd take offence if you didn't drink it. Being able to do your job after consuming far too much wine became a badge of honour. I sometimes saw grown men falling asleep at their desks in the middle of the afternoon.

The camaraderie of the news subs' room at the *Express* was even more legendary. There was a cast of characters, most of whom had nicknames inspired by P G Wodehouse, with catchphrases to match. Even though I heard these names and catchphrases hundreds of times as the characters in question walked in and out of the office, it always made me laugh. It was a testament to the enduring power of the in-joke. Being in on the joke gave me a sense of belonging. It also took me back to the good old days of my dad's gibberish. Well done, comrades – and thanks for letting me be one of the gang. You made it fun to be an invisible mender.

Like sunshine, camaraderie is a joyous word that trips off the tongue. Stolen from the French, it speaks of good fellowship and great companions. And that's what I cherished about the world of print journalism.

Spritzer

My relationship with alcohol started in my mid-teens, when I would wait for my older male pals to buy me a sneaky half of cider or shandy and smuggle it out to the beer garden. When I came of drinking age, I graduated to barley wine – a dark, treacly ale that was cheap, high in alcohol (for a beer) and not usually ordered by young ladies. I did it primarily to shock bartenders and landlords but it was not a sophisticated tipple, so I ditched it in favour of white wine (and, when someone else was footing the bill, champagne). I eventually settled on spritzers as my 'usual'. It was a longer drink that allowed me to fool myself into thinking I wouldn't consume as much alcohol during those long sessions in the pub after work. But a spritzer could still contain a large glass of white wine, with only a few drops of soda to water it down.

There's a gaiety about the word – it conjures up sparkles and freshness. And that was the effect if I had one or two but after three or four it was a different story. That encapsulates my experience with alcohol – it made me exuberant to begin with, then deflated, followed by flat and the opposite of bubbly.

Spritzers accompanied me on my adventures and helped me to forget many of them (thank goodness).

Spritzers helped me to overcome social awkwardness by turning me into a temporary extrovert.

Spritzers allowed me to initiate conversations that I'd never have started while sober.

Spritzers enabled an introvert to become the life and soul of the party.

Spritzers emboldened me – in good and bad ways.

Spritzers – we had fun together but we knew it had to end. We knew we weren't right for each other. At least, you weren't right for me. Spritzers – it's not you, it's me…

In a welcome break from Old French, spritzer is a German/Yiddish word meaning 'to squirt', which fits nicely with my Jewish heritage (on my dad's side). I had my last spritzer at my best friend's funeral (see: Terminal). Shortly after that, me and spritzers (and all forms of alcohol) parted ways. Always loved the word, though – and loved drinking it in. Fizzy word, fizzy (and fuzzy) effect.

Toyboy

Let me state upfront that I *loathe* the word toyboy but it has to feature in my life dictionary because it played such a major part in my midlife story. I'd been aware of it for a while and was dismissive of the idea – I thought the word was demeaning to both men and women. But when

I discovered social media in 2007, everything changed. Remember Myspace? That was my first experience of social media and I joined primarily to reconnect with the musicians I'd known in the 1980s. What I hadn't expected was that, as soon as I signed up, I'd be contacted by younger men looking to hook up with older women.

I'd been single for a while at this point and was shocked that Myspace could be used as a dating site. I was amused by these messages and ignored most of them – but one guy was really persistent. He was Italian. His name was Luca. He was in his early thirties and I'd just turned 50. He kept sending me messages until I agreed to speak to him on the phone. Even though he was bold and suggestive, he made me laugh. He told me there were plenty more young guys out there searching for older women. I was astonished by this revelation, especially as I'd struggled with turning 50 and had started to believe no one would find me attractive, especially as I no longer had the kinky wardrobe to fall back on. I asked him, why me? He said it was because of the look in my eye in my profile photo. I hadn't thought of it as particularly suggestive but apparently it was, certainly in the eye of this particular beholder.

Luca means 'bringer of light' and that's certainly what he did for me. We had a short fling, which ended when he returned to Italy. But it gave me the confidence to explore more connections with younger men, which I did with great gusto by signing up to a dating site called Toyboy Warehouse. To say I was very much in demand was an understatement. I couldn't believe it. I was the proverbial kid in a candy store. After all those years of believing I had to dress up in rubber and leather to be attractive, I felt desired in a way I'd never experienced when I was younger.

Over a period of about six months, I went on dates with

give or take a dozen young men (the youngest was 24) and mostly had an absolute blast (NB: the spritzers helped). They were all delighted to be in the company of a mature woman who had fewer hang-ups than most women of their own age. They knew I wasn't going to badger them about getting married and settling down. On a few occasions I became the Mrs Robinson to their Benjamin but in the end I became tired of the merry-go-round. I dated a couple of guys a couple of times but they weren't looking at me as relationship material. If anything, they were toying with me rather than the other way around.

I was on the verge of calling it a day when I received a message on another dating site (yes, I also set up a profile on a 'normal' dating site) from a man who had clearly taken the time to read my profile rather than just look at my photo (a rare thing, in my experience). Andy was much younger than me – nearly 22 years younger, in fact – but came across as funny, thoughtful and genuinely interested in me as a person. My first thought was that we might become friends. We exchanged emails for a while before we arranged to meet. My first sight of him was at 7.02 pm on 19 December 2007. We'd arranged a rendezvous outside Marks & Spencer on London's Waterloo Station. His train was due at 7.00 pm and his first words to me were: 'Sorry I'm late.'

'Don't be daft,' I said. 'You're only two minutes late.' But what I was thinking was, 'Mate, you're about 25 years late.'

I know it sounds like a romcom cliche but it felt as if I'd known him all my life. The familiarity was immediate. This felt different – and it was. After we'd been on our second date, we knew we were destined to become an item. Yes, there was a big age difference but it didn't feel like that to me or to him. I remember a work colleague asking me how it was going with the toyboy and for a moment I didn't know what he was talking about. I never thought of Andy as a toyboy. He was my partner, my equal. So yes, I hate the word toyboy but can't deny its importance. But it would come back to haunt me in ways I could never have anticipated.

Postscript: The profile photo in question was one taken during a shoot I agreed to do for a feature in the Sunday Express *about the (then) trend for middle-aged women to pose for tasteful semi-nude photo shoots. (I think it was inspired by those saucy Women's Institute calendars.) The photographer stood on a ladder and shot me looking up at him. I was wearing a leather jacket with nothing underneath but it was covering my modesty. However, when I used it on dating websites it wove quite a spell, even without the dominatrix garb.*

Pause for reflection

While recounting my climb to the peak of professional success, this section demonstrates that I was still experiencing a lot of tension between what was going on inside me and what I was doing out in the world – having fun, yes, but still hiding. However, the word 'toyboy' represents the turning point in my story where I was forced into new territory that I hadn't explored before. It was a breakthrough moment that went a long way to regaining the balance that was disrupted by my inciting incident. I finally met a man who loved me unconditionally, which is all I'd ever wanted.

After your series of progressive complications, your challenges and obstacles, what has been the turning point in your life? And which words come to mind that represent that turning point? What territory were you forced into – willingly or unwillingly? What's the story there? And what did you learn from it?

Terminal

There have been two, maybe three women in my life whom I'd describe as best friends but Gill Smith was the one who took the overall title of 'best best friend'. As I mentioned previously, we met in 1983 when I worked for *Record Mirror* and she worked in public relations for a record company. We hit it off straight away and bonded when we went on tour with the electronic pop duo Blancmange. A year later, when I broke up with Tony, whose flat I shared, she took me in. We lived together for a year or so and became inseparable. She later became a music journalist herself and our happiest years were spent working and playing together. However, things took a turn when I started going out with a photographer she disliked intensely. This led to our first period of estrangement, which lasted until after I split up with said boyfriend.

We managed to rebuild the friendship but sadly, years later, we drifted apart again. This time I couldn't see a way back. I was fully prepared to accept that the friendship was over. Then, one day, I received a call from a mutual friend. I could feel it was going to be unwelcome news. She told me that Gill had been diagnosed with non-Hodgkin lymphoma and had been undergoing chemo for some time. Oh, and that Gill's friends had talked her into letting one of them tell me – Gill didn't want to tell me herself. I immediately wrote to Gill, asking if I could visit her. Her reply was swift and devastating: she didn't want to see me. I had let her down too many times. I didn't even know what she meant by this. That night, I sobbed hysterically in Andy's arms. I had to accept once more that I might never see her again. A few months later, I received another call from another mutual friend. This time I was told that Gill's cancer was terminal.

Terminal. Such a solid, immovable object of a word. Terminal. The last stop on the line. The final destination. Terminal. A Latin word relating to the marking of boundaries, it didn't mean 'fatal' until the late 19th century.

Terminal caused Gill to reconsider. She invited me to visit her in hospital. It was as if nothing had happened between us and I'd only seen her the week before. She didn't want to discuss the years of estrangement. She wanted to hear my news. And my news was good: I had a boyfriend and we were engaged to be married. She was thrilled and asked to meet him. Gill had rarely approved of any of the men with whom I'd been involved but she liked Andy. I took that to be the highest form of praise and an excellent omen.

I met up with her a handful of times after that. We never resolved any of our hurts, grievances or misunderstandings. She just wanted me to talk about my life – her way, I presumed, of living vicariously. Then came her move into a hospice. I knew what that meant. One day she called, asking me to come over straight away. I knew what that meant too. Without actually saying the word, she wanted to say goodbye. What do you say to someone who's dying and knows it? Very little, it turns out. You just need to be present with them. That was the last time I saw her. She died three days later, a week or so before her 52nd birthday. I expcrienced survivor's guilt – after all, I was the happiest I'd ever been, looking forward to married life when she had lost her life.

Andy and I set the date for our wedding on 17 April 2010 – Gill's birthday. Terminal couldn't stop us from doing that.

Sober

It was time. I knew it was time. It was partly Gill's death – the passing of a close friend who's the same age as you is clearly going to make you think about your own mortality – but also the recognition that, if I didn't cool it on the spritzer front, I might be storing up health problems for myself later in life. Plus, my fiancé didn't drink alcohol, so I took that as another sign that I should stop drinking.

Alcohol – you and I went on a thrill ride but I knew I had to get off. We'd had an exciting long-term relationship – longer than any of my intimate relationships. But in the end, it was easy. I set the intention to stop drinking alcohol, so I did. I knocked back my final alcoholic beverage (on dry land, that is – see below) at Gill's funeral in 2009. The part that was much, much harder was other people's reactions to my decision to stop drinking alcohol.

It sparked what I call 'drinker's guilt' in some of my friends, leading to the bizarre situation where they would either apologise or ask my permission before ordering another glass. Even my mum couldn't understand why I wouldn't even have a 'little glass of rosé' because in her mind it 'didn't have much alcohol in it'. However, the social implications were harder to deal with. I realised that my drinking buddies were unlikely to continue being buddies once the drinking had been removed from our relationship.

I developed an aversion to public houses – those noisy, often joyless places in which I used to spend many hours of my life believing I was having the best time. I realised that never again would I experience a 'second wind' on a night out and from that point on, I usually wanted to go home by 10 pm (or earlier). I also discovered the inescapable truth that most people become less interesting the more they drink – therefore realising that I had spent more than 40 years being considerably less fascinating than I believed myself to be.

Without the lubricant that had helped me to be sociable ever since I was 16, I felt like that awkward teenager again – the one who always ended up sitting in the corner at parties, feeling overwhelmed and overstimulated. Abandoning alcohol also meant peeling off a few layers of the protection I'd built up over the years. I was no longer consuming a substance that changed my state and distracted me from the sadness at my core.

These days, I avoid parties and find weddings difficult (because guests often use them as an excuse to drink to excess) but persevere for the sake of my friends. It took me a long time to figure out how to fit into social situations and enjoy myself without alcohol but I stuck with it and have been sober ever since. Well, apart from on my honeymoon in 2010. There was so much free champagne on the transatlantic voyage we took on the Cunard liner *Queen Mary II* that I allowed myself a last hurrah – especially as Andy was seasick for the entire six-day crossing to New York.

I recently read an article about the new trend for 'dry dating' – ie not drinking alcohol – at least on the first date (Klein 2022). Apparently, people are discovering they can be more discerning and develop more meaningful connections by sticking to soft drinks. One woman was quoted as saying she lets her hair down and 'shows her more fun side' by drinking on the second date. I find this depressing. Why can she only show her fun side when she drinks alcohol? My biggest fear about not drinking is being seen as a party pooper or a bit boring. Despite being sober, I can still have fun, I can still laugh and I can still misbehave. I just don't get a hangover in the morning or regret my behaviour. I do wish sober didn't also mean serious, sensible and solemn. I guess I'm still judging the word. Maybe I should exchange it for sobriety, a jauntier word with a little more sparkle.

Husband

I proposed to Andy on Leap Year Day (29 February) 2008. It was just a formality – I knew he'd say yes. In hindsight it might seem as if we'd rushed into it but in the two months we'd been dating we'd bonded on a deep level. Plus, we'd decided not to announce our engagement until later that year, so our families wouldn't think we were being impetuous. I waited until Christmas that year to tell my colleagues at the *Sunday Express*. I remember standing next to the news desk with a gaggle of girls around me, all cooing over my engagement ring as if we were recreating scenes from *Pride and Prejudice*. At that precise moment, the editor, Martin, walked past and asked what all the fuss was about. I flashed my ring and told him a little about my fiancé and how we'd met. 'That's the most heart-warming story I've heard in a long time,' he said. 'You must write a first-person piece about it for the first Sunday in January. It'll really cheer people up.' And God knows people needed cheering up, because the financial crash had just happened.

If you google 'true love at 50' you'll see that my article is still on the *Express* website (although you may spot that I decided to tell a slightly different story about who proposed and when). Of all the features I've ever had published in a newspaper or magazine, this is the one that attracted the most affirmative feedback and had the biggest impact. But it seems almost quaint to me now that 50 was regarded as late in life. That article prompted a series of media requests, many of which Andy and I declined, although we did appear in a *Good Housekeeping* feature about unusual pairings as 'the age-gap couple'.

We were married in a former hunting lodge on an idyllic spring day with not a cloud in the sky – or even any trails, as no planes were flying due to a volcanic eruption in Iceland. I wore purple and asked the guests to wear a shade of purple or grey, black and white. Everyone said it was the perfect wedding – and it was. But one of the best things about it for me was that I could finally start saying 'my husband'. I said it as often as possible. I wasn't as bothered about referring to myself as a wife – it was all about my husband. I loved that word. Husband, husband, husband. There was something so comforting and nurturing about the sound of it.

Who would've thought that a former taboo-challenging dominant female entity could form an attachment to such a traditional Old English word meaning 'male head of the household'? Maybe all those years of carousing with pop stars had helped to suppress my innate conservatism (with a small c). The truth is, I adored being married and the fact that I was legally bound to my husband. Maybe it's because I never thought I would get married and that doing it for the first time at 53 was taboo busting in itself. Whatever the truth of the matter, the word husband still feels like a warm hug.

Pavement

It's not a showy word, pavement. It's solid, down to earth and reliable. But that's not why it's on my list. Pavement is here because it played a starring role in a song entitled 'Hold on to Me (I'll Be Here Longer Than the Pavement)', written for me by my husband in the honeymoon phase of our marriage. I'd heard him sing it in our living room with an acoustic guitar and it always made me swell with joy. It hit the mark because I valued the commitment it symbolised – the idea that he would be there for the rest of my life, the foundation stone. Ever since the stroke stole my dad, I'd craved that level of emotional stability. And here it was, in the form of a song. It was perfect. I'd always wanted someone to dedicate a song to me. It gave me a deep feeling of safety and security, the likes of which I hadn't experienced since my early teens.

On my birthday in 2011, almost a year into our marriage, my husband presented me with an extra-special gift: a CD of songs he'd written about our life together, called The Duck Tape (a reference to our pet names for each other – Mr and Mrs Duck). As birthday presents go, it was hard to beat. In fact, I don't think it will ever be beaten. The song was the standout track on the album – now with its fully fleshed-out lyrics and an additional verse that struck to the core of my being. It was deep, meaningful and I still want to keep it private – but in essence, the song was promising that I'd never again feel the emotional pain I'd experienced before I met my husband.

Just over a year later, the pavement crumbled. The fantasy of a firm foundation was just that – a 'candy floss castle', as Gill used to say. I can't listen to the song now – it breaks my heart. I'd like to believe that Andy was 100 per cent sincere when he wrote it but I'll never be sure. At least the song will always be there, even if he's not. Sometimes that which appears solid, down to earth and reliable proves to be anything but. A pavement is built to be walked on but this one walked all over me.

Postscript: Two years after Andy and I separated, I wrote an article for the Telegraph *website about the tough lessons I'd learned from marrying a much younger man. It appeared under the (cringe-inducing) headline: 'How marriage to my toyboy husband (22 years my junior) ended in tears'. It provided an unfortunate bookend to the 'true love at 50' article I wrote for the* Sunday Express. *The entire lifecycle of my relationship was recorded for posterity in national newspapers. 'Don't become the story,' as most journalists say. Unfortunately, I did.*

Divorce

I know what you're thinking. No, surely not… we've only just been celebrating the word husband. But here we are. In order to avoid the apportionment of blame, I waited two years before commencing proceedings (thank goodness this grotesque requirement has now been abandoned). For anyone who hasn't been through it, let me tell you that the process of getting a divorce is dehumanising. You soon realise that the legal bond you entered into in a matter of minutes will take months, if not years, to dissolve and you will be at the mercy of the magistrate's court, which will decide whether or not to grant the divorce in its own sweet time. Men (and probably the odd woman) you've never met will sit in wood-panelled rooms and crawl among the ruins of your most precious, intimate relationship before deciding whether or not you should pay your spouse any money. Luckily, they agreed that I didn't owe my husband anything but the stress of that possibility hung over me for more than a year as we moved inexorably from petition to decree nisi and eventually, after what seemed like an eternity, to decree absolute.

Apparently, some women have divorce parties but

when it was done and dusted, all I felt was overwhelming sadness. At the time, I wrote, 'So this is how it ends. I started this marriage and so I will finish it. He consented to the divorce. By email. Short, formal, to the point. Shorn of emotion. Contained. Distant. As I read his words, a silent sob heaved in my chest and a single tear made its way down my right cheek. I wonder if, beneath the formality of his email, my husband is feeling something similar. I may never know. I don't think my husband ever felt like a husband or understood what it meant. Perhaps part of me never married him. The part that only knows freedom and independence. The part that cannot join in matrimony, holy or otherwise.'

I emailed my ex to inform him that the deed was finally done and he also seemed sad – or, at least, he said he needed time to process the news. I left him to it. We hadn't spoken for some time and after that I didn't need to have any contact with him. I once read an article that said the tragic (and often unacknowledged) part of ending a serious relationship is losing the language you shared together. All those facial expressions, jokes, noises, verbal intimacies and pet names that only the two of you understood. All of that becomes a dead language that will never be spoken again.

I rarely tell anyone I'm a divorcee. It's nothing to be proud of. The divorce word can still activate awful memories and feelings of shame, betrayal, disappointment, desperation and embarrassment. Divorce is something I never wanted and believed would never happen to me. The idea came to me recently that I could never countenance the true meaning of divorce because I was still in love with being married – even though my husband had long since departed with my heart in his suitcase.

If ever there was a word I refused to acknowledge, divorce

was it. Only the reality of it – this heavy word barrelling towards me – forced me into a relationship with it. In the end I was the one who stepped towards it and began an awkward conversation. Of course, it would be me, not my husband – after all, I had been the one to propose, to suggest the wedding date, to do all the organising – so why did I think he would initiate even the slightest eye contact with divorce? I'd taken responsibility for our marriage from day one. He walked away from it without looking back. I realised he'd never taken ownership of it in the first place. I remember his tears on our wedding day and him telling me later that he was crying not because he was marrying me but because all those people were there for him.

The pieces fell into place before I even realised there was a puzzle. It felt as if he'd been playing the role of husband in my play and after a short run he realised he didn't want to act any more. There was nothing I could do or say. He would no longer listen to stage direction. He even looked different – the muscles in his face had relaxed as the tension of playing husband was released. Was I ever really married at all? Yes, in a legal sense but otherwise? Divorce came to collect its debt and I started out on the long, hard road to the dissolution of a dream.

Gratitude

I couldn't end this chapter with divorce. I had to add gratitude because, despite the trials of midlife, I'm still grateful for the experience of meeting, living with and marrying my ex-husband. I have been practising gratitude in some form for many years. Originally I wrote down five things I was grateful for every day but the practice now forms part of my daily meditation. I used to be an inveterate worrier but I believe that maintaining a gratitude practice has helped me to minimise worry and retrain my brain to focus on the positive, even on days when all I can be grateful for is that the sun is shining.

Over the past decade or so, scientists have started to study gratitude and explain why being thankful makes you feel good (Chowdhury 2019). Positive psychologists have a lot to say about the neuroscience of gratitude and its benefits and a white paper put together by the Greater Good Science Center at UC Berkeley (Allen 2018) states, 'A daily diary study found positive relationships between daily feelings of gratitude and feelings of both hedonic [related to pleasure] and eudaimonic [related to meaning and self-realisation] wellbeing.'

It was also through my interest in positive psychology that I discovered an advanced gratitude practice that involves writing a gratitude letter to someone you want to thank – and not sending it to them but reading it out to them in person, the promise being that this would increase your wellbeing as well as the recipient's. So, in 2010, I decided to write Mum a gratitude letter and read it to her when I next visited. I'm sure she thought this was a bit strange – we didn't really do that kind of thing in our family – but she indulged me all the same. When the time came to read the letter, I felt surprisingly nervous. But I knew it was important. Here's how it began:

Dear Mum

We all go through life, with its ups and downs, presuming our family will always be there for us. In particular, we take our parents for granted. So I want you to know that, even though

I might have done so once upon a time, I certainly don't take you for granted now. I always feel grateful when I think of you and how energetic and full of life you still are at almost 83, and how you are still so curious about the world and want to keep learning. You are an inspiration to me.

Tears rolled down my cheeks the entire time I was reading out the letter but Mum sat there, attentive but composed, which was totally in character. I'd rarely seen her cry but she looked pleased and proud and, once she'd made sure I was OK, thanked me as I presented her with the letter, rolled up in a scroll and tied with a ribbon. I'd put money on the fact that she shed a tear once I'd gone. She would later refer to the letter as her 'certificate of motherhood', so I have no doubt that we both benefited from this gift of gratitude.

When she died ten years later I was so glad that I'd taken the opportunity to thank her and tell her how I felt about her as a mother. In fact, the letter formed the basis of my eulogy at her funeral, as well as a blog that I wrote called 'Dear Mum, here's my final gift of gratitude' (2020), which received the largest number of comments I've ever received on my personal blog. It even inspired a couple of my friends to write gratitude letters to their mums and/or dads 'before it was too late'.

Shortly after Mum died and we were able to celebrate her life, I read a beautiful book in which the Dalai Lama and Archbishop Desmond Tutu look back on their long lives to answer the question: how do we find joy in the face of life's inevitable suffering? *The Book of Joy* (2016) states, 'Acceptance means not fighting reality. Gratitude means embracing reality.' And as I move through my sixties, that becomes ever more meaningful to me. Could I even become grateful for grief?

Pause for reflection

Has there been a time in your life when you thought you had it all figured out and realised you didn't? Have you been made redundant or sacked? Did a treasured project fail? Did you end a long-term relationship? Did a partner leave you? And if so, which are the words that have stayed with you? These words may elicit a story that demonstrates your true character and resilience.

While my turning point (meeting and marrying Andy) led to immense joy, this time in my life also brought great sadness and loss – of a close friend and a marriage, among other, smaller losses. The words in this preceding section represent my second crisis point, where I thought I'd reached my happy ever after but discovered it was anything but. All my attempts to return to the halcyon days prior to my inciting incident had failed. Why did I think that would work? But at least I gave up alcohol and appreciated the value of gratitude. Like any true crisis, it revealed my strength of character.

Take your time with this section as it could be a challenging one. Take a breath, look at the prompts and see which ones elicit an immediate response – either a word or a story. Sit down and write (again, in longhand – no typing) more freely than you ever have before. Don't edit or censor yourself – no one else is going to read this (unless you want them to).

- *Which words can transport you back to a time when you felt truly alive?*
- *Which words define your peak professional achievements?*
- *Which words have you relied on to see you through dark times?*

In Your Own Words

- ✎ *Which words tell the story of your crisis point(s)?*
- ✎ *Which words from this stage of life can still make you laugh?*
- ✎ *Which words can still make you cry?*
- ✎ *Which words have you learned the most from?*

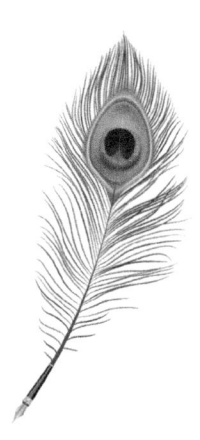

Chapter 6
Wise words

And so we arrive at the part of this book that isn't related to a phase of life. I could've called it 'later life words' but I prefer to associate these words with wisdom. These are the words that have brought you the greatest learning, the deepest acceptance and a profound sense of meaning and purpose. These are the words that you might find in the proverbial pot of gold at the end of the rainbow, the words that help you make sense of everything that has come before, whatever age you've reached.

Wisdom is an Old English word that originally meant knowledge, learning and experience. However, I resonate with the idea that wisdom is nothing more than healed pain, because when you reach this chapter of your story, there's inevitably a lot of pain that has healed – as well as pain that's yet to be healed. I'm hoping that the act of writing about my wise words will help to heal any lingering emotional pain in my heart and soul. I wish that for you too. Wisdom can arrive at any age, so this is as good a time as any to reflect on your wise words.

Grief

I've written about this word many times in the past decade. I needed to figure it out, explore every nuance of it, because it's a word that was hidden in plain sight for so many years. My grief story began in early childhood with the death of my first pet, a budgie called Torchy. It took me a couple of weeks to recover but when our cat Pom Pom was run over by a car it took me much longer to stop feeling sad. Then there was Susan, a girl in my class at school, who died in a freak riding accident when I was 13. She wasn't a close friend but it brought the reality of death uncomfortably close, especially the suddenness of it. Along with my classmates, I experienced a strange kind of collective grief that bordered on hysteria. I don't remember the word grief being used at the time but I felt its emotional punch as well as the underlying sorrow and incomprehension. I understood that you were allowed to feel sad when a person or pet died, even though my parents always shielded me from death (the cloth over the cage concealing the dead budgie; my dad burying the cat in the garden; being told that only adults could go to funerals) and it was never discussed.

And so I arrived at my date with destiny: April Fools' Day 1973. As I mentioned earlier in the book (see: Stroke), I was sweet 16 when my funny, intelligent father had a devastating stroke that left him partly paralysed and dependent on my mother. He was only 46, in the prime of life. His physical disability was hard enough to deal with but his personality changed too, in a way that was hard to articulate to anyone outside my immediate family. Like many people who suffer brain injuries, he was much less rational, more easily moved to tears; he seemed less sophisticated and much sillier (but not in a fun way). He had a much shorter attention span and stumbled over his words (which I later learned was aphasia). In her less sympathetic moments, Mum called him her 'fourth child'. I quickly came to realise that he could no longer play the role of father in any way that was meaningful to me, a girl on the cusp of womanhood. It made me angry that I had to look after him when he should've been looking after me. I was in shock for months after it happened. It was as if a big black hole had opened up inside me. I had no words to describe how I was feeling, so I didn't talk to anyone about it. We – me, my mum, older sister and younger brother – just got on with life, each frozen in our own ways, as if a curse had turned us to ice.

I resonated with a profoundly moving piece by Jennifer Senior in *The Atlantic* (2021) about a family dealing with the loss of a son and brother on 9/11. The family spoke to a grief counsellor, who told them each family member would grieve differently. Imagine you're all at the top of a mountain, she told them, but you all have broken bones, so you can't help each other. You each have to find your own way down. That metaphor went some way to describing how our family coped with Dad's stroke. To this day, I still haven't spoken to my siblings in any depth about how they got down the mountain.

It took years of soul searching, therapy and counselling before I realised what was really going on. The wound could never heal because I was still staring into an open grave. I had to see through the pain. Even though he was still alive, my dad's ability to be a functioning father had died when I was 16 – and I'd never grieved. I never even knew it was grief that I'd been feeling for all those years, sometimes spiking into gnawing despair but always a background sadness, even in happier times. This was a revelation to me, so I spent hours poring over books about grief and how to deal with it. It hadn't occurred to me that we all experience grief, even after a small loss. And that loss isn't always about people or pets – we can feel grief after the loss of hope, a dream or an expectation.

My family didn't talk much about 'difficult' emotions. We were fluent in laughter and humour and often used both to mask those difficult emotions. I could count on the fingers of one hand how many times I'd seen my mum cry – she kept her tears out of sight. One enduring childhood memory is of me standing outside my parents' bedroom, holding my dad's hand, and him telling my sobbing mum through the closed door that she was upsetting me. I was more confused than upset but received the message that day that not only was sadness a private experience, it was also something to be ashamed of that you inflicted on other people at your peril.

All of this fresh understanding about grief helped me to break through to a new level of compassion for myself. There were plenty of tears but they were good, healthy tears, not wallowing in self-pity tears. I'd managed to peel off a layer of grief but there were many more to come. By the time I was 50, I'd peeled enough of them away to connect to joy – and that's when I met my future husband.

My work wasn't done, though. It took almost four more years and many breathwork sessions before I was able to give myself permission to dive into the depths of my grief and that's when I found out what it was made of – how much fear was there, how much anger, how much sadness. Right at the bottom of it, there was rage. And I'd told myself the biggest lie about this rage – that it would destroy me. I'll never forget the day I gave myself permission to feel that rage. It lasted a couple of minutes at most and when it was over, I stood up and said, 'Fancy that, I survived.'

But it seems as if grief has always been around the corner, waiting for me. My dad died suddenly when he was 73; two close acquaintances committed suicide; my best friend Gill died of cancer; my marriage ended after only two years; my sister-in-law passed away after a long illness; then my mum – the rock of our family – began her slow descent into physical frailty and cognitive decline and died during the pandemic.

I didn't want to meet grief again in this book. I put it off, I resisted. But we've always been companions. We've walked side by side for most of my adult life. British psychiatrist Colin Murray Parkes wrote in his book *Bereavement: Studies of Grief in Adult Life* (1972), 'The pain of grief is just as much a part of life as the joy of love; it is, perhaps, the price we pay for love, the cost of commitment.' I believe and accept that. I just wish I'd been properly introduced to grief at an early age, when I had the chance to grow with it. It would've helped me make sense of the world and my inner life. The word was always there but wasn't available to me in any meaningful way until much later. When I read Cariad Lloyd's book *You Are Not Alone* (2023) I felt a lot of compassion for her, losing her dad at 15. But I also felt envious that she knew she was grieving. I didn't. Grief was a mystery to me when I was 16 and it certainly wasn't part of my vocabulary.

The root of the word is in Old French and originally meant grievance, injustice and misfortune; it didn't come to mean intense sorrow and mental suffering until the 13th century – but modern grief retains its heaviness and gravity. I understand grief so much better now – in fact, I seek its counsel. I recently read another book about it, David Kessler's *Finding Meaning* (2019), which suggests that the final (sixth) stage of grief is, indeed, finding meaning. Yes, that fits; I'm always searching for meaning. I never thought I'd say it but I'm not angry with grief any more. I'm actually grateful. Grief gave me emotional depth and intelligence. It deepened my sensitivity and gave me the chance to develop what I think of as 'early onset wisdom'.

Solitude

Despite the origin of this word (from the Latin *solitudo*, meaning loneliness), there's an important distinction to be drawn between solitude and loneliness. You can find peace and comfort in being alone but there's none of that in feeling lonely. I prefer the framing of being alone as 'all one' and therefore not needing another to complete the picture.

Solitude is my comfort zone, my default. Ever since I moved into my first flat at the age of 19 (a room in a shared house where I rarely saw my housemates), I've experienced many years of solitude. I've moved in with boyfriends for a few years here and there, shared a flat with a friend and, of course, lived with my husband for a few years but have lived alone for long stretches.

In my solitude I've discovered many companions – imagination, creativity, fantasy, compassion, reflection… I've always had close friendships but having my safe solo space has always been important – even vital – to my ability to function. However – and here's the rub – there's a limit to how much solitude I can endure. Give me too much of it (hello, lockdown) and it becomes a prison. Everything I discover while in solitude needs to be expressed to other human beings, otherwise it remains locked inside. The exquisite agony of being an introvert is the knife-edge balance you need to maintain between alone time (to recharge) and connection with others. Too much of one and not enough of the other can become distressing. I've also experienced the pain of feeling lonely while in a relationship. Solitude is far preferable to that.

Many renowned artists and writers have extolled the virtues of solitude and its creative value. Keats saw it as a conduit to truth and beauty; fellow poet Elizabeth Bishop believed that everyone should experience at least one period of prolonged solitude in their life; and Susan Sontag wrote in 1977, 'One can never be alone enough to write. To see better' (see Popova 2012). And yes, solitude has always helped me to focus on and deepen my writing.

As I move through my sixties, I value solitude more and more. I know Mum struggled when Dad died and she was on her own for the first time in her life. I cope with being alone much better than she did. I accept it, even though I don't always choose it. I was more than happy to surrender my solitude when I got married. I wanted to be with my husband for the rest of my life. But it seems that solitude didn't want to let me go, so here we are, back together again. Is it forever? I hope not, but solitude is like a pair of comfy slippers. I can slip back into it whenever I need to – even when I yearn to put on my stilettos, albeit metaphorically.

Unspoken

Such a strange word, unspoken – it refuses to speak. What it does communicate is… silence – that which isn't expressed in words. It implies being gagged, or not having permission to speak, or hiding what needs to be said, or a tacit set of rules that have never been explicitly agreed upon.

Unspoken: all those thoughts and feelings stuffed inside, never given a voice.

Unspoken: words that may never be heard.

Such a sad word, unspoken. What has been left unsaid? Such a secretive word. What has been deliberately omitted? The grief that I've written about in this book was unspoken for many years. It didn't have a chance to voice itself.

The misgivings my husband had about our marriage were unspoken. Many of the deeper feelings I've struggled to make sense of have remained unspoken, embedded in my mind and body.

Such a curious word, unspoken.

When I became a human potential coach in 2011, I decided to brand my website The Pearl Within – a metaphor for the precious qualities we have within us that have formed around and because of our pain, like the pearl that encloses a foreign body in an oyster shell. I believe that pain can be transformed into something beautiful if only we could risk breathing through it and talking about it. I believe that this pain is often caused by suffering in silence and that by voicing the pain we can break that silence and end our suffering.

So many of us leave so many words unspoken. Maybe some of them are better off unsaid but others could have been music to someone's ears. Such an imprisoning word, unspoken. Let it not be said.

Pause for reflection

After the drama of my midlife words, my first set of wise words feels calmer, more thoughtful and even poetic. They reflect a period in my life when I went on a deep dive into personal growth and development, trying to make sense of what had come before and confronting difficult truths about the choices I'd made and the hopes and dreams I was forced to let go of. It was during this time that I had to make a critical decision: was I going to withdraw and wait for my wounds to heal or once again push myself to go out into the world and make myself (and therefore my wounds) visible?

Have you had to make a critical decision? It may or may not have been your darkest hour but your choice of wise words may well come from a point in your life when you lost hope or faith. What is that story? What did you learn in that moment that will serve others?

In a classic narrative structure, this is the point in the story when all seems lost. My mind immediately goes to the moment in *The Lord of the Rings* when Frodo is being consumed by the darkness of the ring and doesn't have the energy to walk another step towards Mount Doom. So his faithful friend Samwise has to carry him. In my story, having made my critical decision, I soon started to see the light of dawn and allowed others to carry me.

Spoken

Ah – the relief! An antidote to the unspoken – that which most definitely *is* said. Shout it from the rooftops! Spoken is here! Too late, unspoken – the word is out! I wouldn't usually sprinkle exclamation marks (known in the newspaper trade as 'screamers') through my writing but the release of energy is palpable. I had to express it on the page, especially after the straitjacket of unspoken. After all, words are vibrations – once out, they're out, so watch out. I have spoken! There's a dynamic quality to the word – action has been taken to communicate. Feelings have been expressed; ideas shared.

In the world of words, spoken is the companion of written. And this is the story of how I came to travel from the written to the spoken word.

Having been a wordsmith for so long, it was never on my radar to dabble in the spoken word. Throughout my years with a high-profile byline and then afterwards in the role of invisible mender, I didn't need to be the spoken one. My only experience of public speaking had been in 1988, when I was editor of the pop magazine *Record Mirror*. I'd been invited to speak at the Oxford Union, the most prestigious university debating society in the country (if not the world). Accustomed to entertaining the great and the good, who usually took part in worthy political debates, the debating society occasionally injected some light relief. The debate to which I'd been invited was one of the 'fun' ones. The motion I'd been asked to speak to was 'Has rock 'n' roll lost its balls?' It's a question that I'd go on to answer in the affirmative. I prepared by writing a script, which I planned to read out to the assembly. I didn't really think about it much more than that, so when I rocked up to Oxford University that afternoon, it quickly dawned on me what I'd signed up for. The chairman of the debating society asked me to sign the visitors' book – a leather-bound tome containing the signatures of prime ministers, presidents and other notables. And little old me.

When I was escorted into the debating chamber, I discovered it was a miniature replica of the House of Commons, complete with a dispatch box (a training ground for many British politicians, including Boris Johnson). Feeling like a complete imposter, I shuffled onto a bench, waiting my turn like a witness at a murder trial. When it was time for me to speak, I stood next to the dispatch box, gripping my script and reading my argument to the best of my ability while making little or no eye contact with the assembled students. When the ordeal was over, I scuttled back to my seat and vowed never to do any public speaking again (although my joke about the pop band Bros did get a laugh and my side won the debate, meaning that rock 'n' roll officially 'lost its balls' in 1988).

I stayed in my writing and editing comfort zone for the next 25 years.

So what tempted me back into the spoken word? It was a chance encounter with an effervescent force of nature called Sarah Lloyd-Hughes at a party I wanted to leave. (I did leave, after about 20 minutes, knowing I'd met the person I needed to meet.) It was at one of the workshops run by Sarah in the early days of her company, then called Ginger Public Speaking, that I first experienced the power of the spoken word. At the end of the event, she invited two or three participants to jump up and speak spontaneously for two minutes. I was one of them – speaking about how I'd been performing all my life and that this was the first time I'd shown up as my authentic self. After those two minutes, I burst into tears – the kind of dramatic release that only occurs when you speak your truth. I had spoken! No more hiding!

Don't get me wrong – I still loved the written word but the spoken word intrigued me. I instinctively knew that speaking was something I needed to do more of and get better at. So, I signed up for a couple of Ginger's courses, including the Inspiring Speakers' Programme, a six-month journey into the spoken word, culminating in a grand finale where I would deliver a ten-minute talk to an invited audience.

You could say that the word spoken saved my life. My emergence as a speaker coincided with the separation from my husband and rescued me from the silence of heartbreak. I rejected the unspoken and chose to speak. My finale speech was titled 'There's No Such Thing as an Ordinary Life' and it won me the audience's People's Choice award. One human gestation period later, I was reborn as a public speaking coach and trainer, working for Sarah at Ginger, fully inhabiting the spoken word and advocating its power to others. Spoken liberated me, fulfilled me, gave me fresh purpose and an unexpected new career path. That's why it has to be one of my wise words.

Author

My journey through the written word has taken me from writer to editor to author. The idea of writing a memoir first emerged in the late 1990s, when my then boyfriend James suggested a wider audience might be interested in my stories about being a music journalist in the 1980s. I thought people might enjoy reading my old interviews, interspersed with social and personal commentary, so I started doing some research. Unfortunately, I'd saved very few original copies of the music papers in which my writing had been published so I had to spend many hours in the British Library repository in north London, trawling through leather-bound volumes of *Sounds* and *Record Mirror*.

What followed was a long and arduous process of stitching together my memories with what had been published – but it was one I fully committed to, despite the fact that much of it felt like therapy, as I came face to face with a younger version of myself that I barely recognised and often felt ashamed of. I'd never attempted to write a book, so even though I was writing chronologically about real events, it felt like climbing a mountain – especially when my dad died suddenly of a heart attack in November 2000.

After a six-month hiatus, I picked it up again – then came to another creative halt in the bewildering aftermath of 9/11. I realised that in order to reach the summit I'd have to temporarily give up my part-time job at the *Sunday Express* to focus on finishing a first draft. The subsequent lack of distraction gave me the opportunity to revisit old haunts in my mind and I frequently emerged feeling haunted. I'd underestimated how challenging it would be to dig through memories – some of which I'd suppressed. Who was this girl? Why did she do those things? But slowly, slowly… the peak came into view. I finished the first draft – a massive 150,000-word outpouring.

My next – not inconsiderable – task was to find a literary agent. I contacted a few who I thought might be interested in a music industry memoir, to no avail. Then Gill said she would introduce me to her agent (after her stint as a music journalist she became the editor of a teen magazine and had gone on to become a writer of teen and romantic fiction). I sent in my draft and waited. Eventually the agent got back to me and said she was interested in taking me on. There was one proviso, which was to cut 50,000 words – particularly the interview transcripts – and make it even more personal, without oversharing. This puzzled me but I did what she asked.

I slashed and I burned and eventually produced a second draft with which my agent was satisfied. Then she began the long, drawn-out, somewhat arcane process of pitching my memoir – *Hit Girl: My Bizarre Double Life in the Pop World of the Eighties* – to major publishers. As anyone who's had an agent knows, it can often be months before you hear anything after sending a manuscript to a publisher. Eventually, responses started to trickle in – a 'no, not for us' here, a 'great fun, but won't fit on our list' there – plenty of encouraging noises but no one was prepared to publish it. The most disheartening reaction was from the publisher who claimed that no one wanted to read about a writer who had interviewed celebrities – they wanted to read about celebrities, in their own words. And maybe I'd be interested in ghostwriting? No, I wouldn't. They were effectively telling me my life wasn't interesting enough because I wasn't a 'name writer'. After about 18 months, having exhausted every publishing house in the book, including small independents, we gave up. My memoir was left on the shelf – and it's still there.

You can't claim to be an author if your work hasn't been published, so, many years later, I wrote a short book about personal storytelling. What motivated me to do this was my belief (first aired publicly in my award-winning talk) that none of us are ordinary and we all have an extraordinary story to share. And it's only now that I've realised that this belief stemmed from my experience of my memoir being rejected by publishers as not interesting enough because I wasn't famous.

In 2015, I self-published my little ebook *Dig for the Story in Your Soul: #StoryWisdom to Help You Author an Authentic Life* (still available on Amazon, a snip at £5.99). An unwieldy title, perhaps but I managed to fit the word author in there. I also delighted in including 'a word from the author' just after the foreword, which explained that the book was based on a collection of graphics I'd created for social media using the hashtag #StoryWisdom. I created the first one in less than 30 seconds – 'We all have an extraordinary story to share. Let your voice be heard.' I subsequently produced hundreds of graphics, which I shared every weekday on social media. The book featured 52 #StoryWisdom reflections, one for each week of the year, with accompanying questions to prompt story ideas. It represented the distilled essence of my knowledge and thinking about the power of personal storytelling at that time. #StoryWisdom week one is still my favourite: 'There's no such thing as an ordinary life. You matter. Your story matters.'

So now I *am* an author. I published a book that features many of my personal stories. It garnered several five-star reviews. I think it would make a good companion to this, my first 'proper' book. Maybe there will be a third book. Maybe it will be the 'lost memoir'.

The roots of the word author are in the 14th century, when the act of creating something was seen as a purely masculine activity, associated with the father. Author is also the root of the word authority. These days, whatever your gender, being an author automatically confers expertise – even if it's merely expertise in your own experience.

Pause for reflection

Let's rest here for a moment as I reach the climax of my story so far. As I see it, I've now fulfilled the 'quest' activated by my inciting incident and restored balance in many ways, including writing about my life. It's the only way I can make sense of what I've experienced. By giving my life story shape and structure, my brain can find patterns and connections, thereby creating a high degree of personal meaning.

Can you identify the climax of your story so far? Or are you still working your way towards it? The climax of your story might be the moment of maximum tension or conflict. Mine wasn't – it felt like more of a release and resolution. Perhaps your words will lead you to a resolution too and you'll end up with a coherent life story.

There has been plenty of research into narrative coherence (defined as the extent to which an individual is able to construct coherent accounts of their autobiographical memories). A study conducted in Belgium (Vanaken et al 2021) looked at how narrative coherence impacted emotional wellbeing during the Covid pandemic. The scientific jury's still out on this one but my experience is that it can be hugely beneficial to feel that your story is coherent and makes sense. But I also know that the human brain won't hesitate to confabulate in order to make sense of an experience. According to an article in *Scientific American* (Konnikova 2012), our minds form cohesive narratives out of disparate elements all the time and 'If we're not sure, we make it up – or rather, our brain does, without so much as thinking about asking our permission to do so.' This is why we're all unreliable narrators – our brains will fill in the gaps of a story, often with events that never happened.

This raises a series of questions. Can I trust any of my memories? Did any of this really happen in the way I remember? Am I exaggerating? My answers would be: probably not; memory is not like a video camera (Northwestern University 2014); and *sometimes* – but it's not my fault. The brain reframes and edits events to fit your current map of the world. So next time you go for a walk down memory lane, remember the words of the late neurologist Oliver Sacks: 'Frequently, our only truth is narrative truth – the stories we tell each other and ourselves – the stories we continually re-categorise and refine.' (Popova 2013)

The most important part is to identify the *emotional* truth of your story – one that doesn't rely *solely* on the facts as you remember them. The way you're interpreting your story *right now* and how you feel about it is where you'll find meaning. Does your story *feel* coherent? Do you *feel* the truth of it? Search for that wisdom.

Intuition

For me, the composition of this word – in (inner) followed by tuition (teaching/learning) – has always been key to its meaning. Intuition is all about listening to the wisdom within – that still, small voice that you can only hear if you dial down the trash metal volume of your thoughts and inner dialogue. I suspect I trusted my intuition before I went to school, where left-brained tuition drummed it out of me. Teachers' voices joined my parental conditioning and it was no longer easy to hear that inner wisdom or believe it was there.

I've had a bumpy journey with intuition. It has taken me a long time to trust it again. There were many times when I believed I was following my intuition, especially when it came to relationships with men, only to realise I was following something quite different – usually my fantasy of what could be. I blamed intuition for my failings and eventually tuned it out. One of the reasons why I studied astrology was because it codified intuition. As long as I had my astrology books, I could interpret a birth chart without having to rely on my own intuition.

Gill was the intuitive one. She was a clairvoyant who studied to be a medium. She could read tarot cards – I couldn't. Or at least I believed I couldn't. It was much later in life that I started to trust my flashes of insight, especially when a reiki teacher encouraged me to 'go with the first' and not immediately dismiss a thought or feeling, however nonsensical it might seem to my reasoning mind. Thus I was able to rebuild my trust in intuition and the still, small voice would get slightly louder or be easier to hear in meditation and amid the cacophony of thoughts. I started to go with the first and found that my first thoughts and feelings resonated with others.

I've used intuition as a tool to author this book – often using creative writing exercises (automatic or stream of consciousness writing) to connect to each of my chosen words so that I feel I'm 'being written' rather than thinking about what to write. I have a good relationship with intuition these days. It's my constant companion, especially when I'm coaching a client or listening to someone's personal story. When I'm helping people to find their voice in the written or spoken word, I begin with my intuition (feeling into what needs to be said and what wants to emerge) and then move towards precision – choosing specific language and thinking about structure, clarity and editing.

Intuition emerged in the 15th century with a theological meaning. The insight it described was considered to be religious in nature. Intuition is such a beautiful, intangible thing – a window on the spiritual world, perhaps even a divine intervention. Always within, intuition will never let you go without.

Precision

Ooh, precision – you make me shiver with delight. I'm constantly impressed by your exactitude and accuracy. I love the way you go straight to the heart of the matter and remove the waffle. You have the quality of a razor-sharp knife – the expensive chef's variety, ready to slice and dice with maximum efficiency.

Ooh, precision – you can cut me off any time you like...

OK, I'm getting carried away here but over the years I've developed the skill of linguistic precision. I've spent thousands of hours poring over page proofs and later computer screens, correcting grammar and punctuation, meticulously editing copy to enhance its clarity and impact and writing smart headlines that fit into their allotted space without repeating any words in the intro.

However, there have been times when I haven't been precise in my communication, when there have been misunderstandings with loved ones. I'm only human. But in the world of words, I've come to value precision as much as intuition – and that's why I use them both, in service of each other.

Precision is the best mate of clarity. According to *The New Yorker* (Overbey 2011), writer Vladimir Nabokov once said, 'A writer should have the precision of a poet and the imagination of a scientist.' I'm not a numbers person but for me, one of the attractions of astrology is its numerical precision. I find it incredible that you can predict the position of every planet to the exact degree hundreds of years into the future.

Ooh, precision – you give me a frisson of control.

I don't think precision is fashionable (its sibling concision even less so) but I find anyone who values it is more likely to be a kindred spirit. Much like simplicity, precision is difficult to achieve – you have to work at it. Being vague is easy but imprecision is a word that's unlikely to be used by those who are careless with their language.

The original meaning of the word is 'freedom from inessential elements', as it's described in the Online Etymology Dictionary. Like Michelangelo seeing his David in a block of marble, I enjoy uncovering and shaping the essential elements in a piece of writing. Ooh, precision – you make me feel as if I've sculpted word statues that will be my legacy.

Clarity

Just before I sat down to write about clarity, I was listening to one of my favourite podcasts, *The Daily* from *The New York Times*. The production team delivers bite-sized clarity on a daily basis, interspersed with human interest stories that often move me to tears. This particular podcast, broadcast in May 2020, was no exception. The presenter, Michael Barbaro, was interviewing one of their reporters, Audra Burch, about the horrific killing of George Floyd. Barbaro asked her simple questions in order to understand the sequence of events, teasing out a clear narrative on behalf of his listeners. At the end, emotionally exhausted by the story, the reporter said that, after such a tragedy, sometimes all you can do is sit still. She ended by saying, 'I fight for clarity. I think that's the only thing you can fight for after something like this happens.'

That final statement, coming after such a gut-wrenching story, is what made me cry. I'll never understand what it feels like to be a person of colour but I can resonate with Audra Burch's passionate desire to bring clarity to the world and her willingness to fight for it. I guess, in my own small way, I fight for clarity as well – clarity in the written and spoken word. Like precision, clarity cuts to the core of the matter. There's no space for doubt when clarity is around. There's a radiance about clarity – as if you're waking up for the first time and seeing the world in HD. The origin of the word suggests a meaning that's even more transcendent than that – brilliant, glorious, a many-splendoured thing.

There's nothing like that moment of blinding clarity when everything falls into place and there's absolutely no doubt in your mind what needs to be said or what has to happen. It can sometimes feel like a breaking point. One Sunday in June 2012, my husband announced he was going out to see his friends and I challenged him, asking why he didn't want to stay at home with his wife. He didn't explain. He left the house anyway. Moments later, I called his mobile, demanding an explanation. He finally agreed to come back and talk. I watched out of the window as he walked back up the hill from the station car park. I'll never forget that sight. It was like a moment in a TV drama – the moment before everything changes. I knew that the conversation that was about to take place would provide a level of clarity that both of us had been resisting for a long time.

Back in our living room, he looked at me with steely eyes that I hadn't seen before and said, without apparent emotion, 'I've changed my mind about wanting children.' Being the age-gap couple, we'd had many conversations about children before we got married and he'd always said he'd rather be with me than have children. I blurted out something about fostering or adoption before he continued, 'No, you don't understand. I want to have children with a woman of my own age.' The power of that truth bomb made it abundantly clear: our marriage was over. It took me a year to accept it but that was the moment of blinding clarity.

I had to take a 24-hour break after writing those two preceding sentences, as the experience of remembering that moment can still knock me off my feet.

Clarity: you can be brutal but also beautiful. I fight for clarity in my thinking and in my emotions. I fight for clarity in every sentence I write and every sentence I edit for other people. I get such a thrill when I fight for someone else to gain clarity and they find it.

Clarity: you are a double-edged sword. You help me cut to the chase but sometimes I get sliced in the process. But even if I occasionally bleed – clarity, I will still fight for you.

Contentment

I remember watching Melvin Bragg's 2003 documentary series *The Adventure of English* and being surprised to discover that the English language nearly disappeared from these shores when William the Conqueror pronounced that the English court, government and upper class would speak only French. That's why as many as 45 per cent of our words are of French origin and contentment is one of them.

Its original (now obsolete) meaning was the satisfactory payment of a debt. But I can see the connection with the current meaning (being satisfied with present conditions); what I was owed has been returned to me and it feels good.

I'm also intrigued by the notion that contentment is passive while satisfaction is active. As Mick Jagger informed us back in the 1960s, you can try as hard as you like to get yourself some satisfaction but you'll probably fail. Contentment, however, isn't something you try to achieve – it just *is*. Contentment is the acceptance of what is without grasping for more – and finding the silver lining within.

Contrary to the picture I've painted with some of the words I've chosen, I have experienced contentment in my life and hope to experience much more. But happiness, I find, is fleeting and often dependent on external events and other people. In contrast, contentment can be experienced in solitude. In fact, at this stage in my life, contentment = solitude + gratitude.

Lockdown gave me the opportunity to look for silver linings and thankfully I've found many. One of the biggest has been finding contentment in the act of writing and reflecting on my life. I still have moments when I yearn for love and companionship but that can throw me into a state of dissatisfaction. Contentment brings me back to my centre, feeling grateful for what I have rather than longing for what I don't have. Buddha is credited with saying 'Health is the greatest gift, contentment the greatest wealth' – and life in lockdown brought that home to me in a powerful way. Rather than the pursuit of happiness, I will henceforth focus on the calm cultivation of contentment.

Soul

I don't like to use the term now but, for a few years at least, my husband was close to being my 'soulmate' – despite saying, after we'd separated, that I didn't have enough soul music in my collection. I explained to him that I grew up listening to Motown on the radio – it was the soundtrack to my childhood and early teens – and even though I didn't own the albums, it didn't signify a lack of respect or love for the music. I've just never been a record collector. But I adored Prince. From the moment he stepped on stage at the Lyceum in 1981, his first-ever London gig, I became obsessed with him. The Prince and the Revolution gig at Wembley Arena in 1988 remains the best live show I've ever seen (and I've seen quite a few). It was a soulful experience that lifted me up and put me on a spiritual high for days. When I was a music journalist, I encountered a lot of snobbery about soul music, mostly among a clique of male writers who looked down their noses at me because I wrote about pop, which they considered to be disposable and less culturally significant.

I didn't reclaim the word soul until much later in life, when I opened myself up to deeper spiritual work and came to understand the true nature of the soul as that which is indestructible – the energetic essence that's carried into different incarnations after physical death. I trust that I have a soul but my soul is not me in any sense of what I understand 'me' to be. It's perhaps a consciousness that's within me but outside my conscious control. I can 'feel it in my soul' while being unable to identify where my soul is located. I can 'dig for the story in my soul' as I advised others to do in my ebook and instinctively know what that means, without being able to describe it in literal terms.

Soul was originally an Old English (Anglo-Saxon) word meaning the spirit or essence of a being, the life force, and predated the arrival of Christianity in England in the late 6th century. And we're still arguing about what it really means in the 21st century. Soul, you are a conundrum, a mystery, a will o' the wisp. You are one of the wisest words I could ever imagine, even though your wisdom often feels out of reach. I hope, in the time I have left in this incarnation, that I will reach an understanding of what a soul truly is, inspired by a quotation attributed to the Sufi poet Rumi: 'The desire to know your soul will end all other desires.'

Surrender

This word has been confronting me since I was 16, when the 'hand of God' intervened in my life. Since then, it has revisited me many times. It has always pointed me in the direction it wants me to head in rather than the direction I wanted to take. It's a slippery word that I've struggled to get a handle on. I've been conditioned to believe it means to give up, wave the white flag – cowardice, weakness. But the longer I live and the more it revisits me, the more I realise the need to let go of that conditioning.

I've come to understand that surrender is a state of grace. It means acceptance of what is – whatever that may be. It means giving up the desires, wants and needs of my ego. It means yielding when I want to push or direct. It means acknowledging a higher power – something unknowable and transcendent that's much better at directing the course of my life than I am.

Even though I don't think of myself as an artist, I once painted surrender. There were swirls of glorious pink and purple around the letters. It looked sensuous and beautiful.

Even the sound of surrender is a hint to its true meaning.

S-s-s-s-s-s-surrender.

Elongate that s… and slip and slide into the render.

For so long I'd say I didn't know how to 'do' surrender. I even bought a book about the art of letting go in order to learn how to do it. How surrender must have laughed!

You don't 'do' surrender – surrender does you.

In his book *The Power of Now* (1997), Eckhart Tolle writes, 'Surrender is the simple but profound wisdom of yielding to rather than opposing the flow of life.' After a lifetime of pushing and trying to make things happen, that was such a relief to hear. Surrender, then, surely must be a gateway to the divine. Whenever I heard the saying 'let go and let God', it used to annoy me, as if my agency and free will were being taken away. But I realised it's a healthier, happier and more fruitful way to live – whatever God means to you. The key is in knowing when to surrender and when to act – and that's something I'm learning all the time. I don't want to be seen as passive but there's something about letting life happen to you rather than trying to make life happen that shifts your entire outlook. Another Old French word, surrender originally meant to give something up or back – and I guess it still does. Surrender, I believe, will always be a work in progress for me. Life will keep offering up opportunities for me to let go, and maybe even (God forbid) let God (see: God).

As part of her inspiring Art Meets Poetry project, my talented artist friend Furrah Syed invited me to submit a piece of my writing that she would then respond to with a painting. What I sent her was a version of the above – 'On Surrender'. In the notes that accompanied an image of her response, Furrah explained, 'I wanted to create a background of yellow (our existence) then two flows, one representing your energy (green and blue; colours of life) and the other the guidance from above/God (yellow, red and gold). I had a very strong image of surrender being depicted as the darkest colour – black. I wanted there to be solid and very stark shapes taking centre stage but with variations; some stop the flow of your journey in life, some allow more or less of you to proceed towards the guidance of God. This piece is unlike anything I have created before but I feel it honestly represents your words and sentiments.' As someone who has always been able to express myself in words but rarely in any other medium, it was a privilege to see Furrah's interpretation. She gifted me the painting and for me it captures the essence and energy of the word surrender in such a meaningful way – but without words.

Serenity

Ah – serenity: the handmaiden of contentment. It comes from the Latin *serenus*, meaning clear, calm, peaceful. People often describe me as calm and I'm rather good at appearing to be unruffled. But sometimes calm can mask a troubled mind; serenity, however, remains untroubled and unclouded. I love the sound of the word and its association with clarity. Serenity will always make me think of the famous Serenity Prayer, originally written by American theologian Reinhold Niebuhr in 1951: 'God, grant me the serenity to accept the things I cannot change, courage to change the things I can, and the wisdom to know the difference.' That speaks to surrender, as well as knowing when to act.

When I was a music journalist, I was lucky enough to

be invited by a Japanese record label to visit Japan. I was taken on a tour from Tokyo to Osaka and Kyoto that included a visit to a beautiful, minimalist stone garden. It was difficult not to feel serene while sitting in one of these 'dry landscape' gardens, which are designed to imitate the essence of nature and serve as an aid to meditation. I think I'd appreciate it much more now than I did then, as I was still living in the fast lane and was more excited about jumping on the bullet train than contemplating a bunch of rocks and gravel, however attractively arranged. Oh, to be back in Kyoto, pondering the meaning of existence. Now I do it in the privacy of my own garden (well, patio balcony), where a large Buddha watches over me. Again, serenity is a state I aspire to rather than achieve all the time – after all, I'm only human. Unlike...

God

Oh God... I've been dreading this one, even though I knew I couldn't avoid it. Just like the origin of the word, my relationship with God has been complicated. The complications began long before I was born. My parents were determined not to indoctrinate their three children with any religious dogma. My mum had been confirmed as a child and identified as a Christian (but rarely went to church), while my dad, being a scientist, identified as agnostic (and sometimes atheist). However, there was a painful story at the root of this. My paternal grandfather was part of a large Jewish family and had been the only sibling not to marry a Jewish woman. This was scandalous at the time, as the Jewish lineage is passed down through the mother. In fact, my grandparents split up for a while due to family pressure, before reuniting and marrying. So you might imagine that this would make it easier for my dad to marry whomever he chose – but no, my grandparents wanted him to marry a Jewish girl (presumably to atone for the 'sins' of his father). When my parents started dating, Dad's parents didn't approve and Mum told me she never felt welcome. But, like his father before him, my dad insisted on his own choice of wife. My poor mum had to have a register office wedding at a time when such things carried a stigma, simply because my paternal grandparents refused to attend a church service. This intolerance and hypocrisy resulted in my dad rejecting religion altogether and my mum withdrawing from it.

God didn't really feature in my childhood until I chose to attend Sunday school at a local free church, where my friend's dad was a teacher. Even then I remember sitting through the vicar's sermons and feeling completely bored and disengaged. God wasn't speaking to me then. However, I did love the Bible stories we studied at Sunday school. After that, God became part of the curriculum and something that had to be tolerated as part of religious education. I was taught that 'In the beginning was the Word, and the Word was with God, and the Word was God.' None of my teachers were willing to explain this to me in a way that I could understand. Even now, you can find a thousand different interpretations.

It wasn't that I actively didn't believe in God, just that I never really thought about God that much at all. 'He' said nothing to me about my life. Not until my dad had a stroke. Then I did start to believe in God, because I needed to be angry with Him. But I still prayed to Him to save my dad's life. It seems that He listened because my dad survived for another 27 years. I didn't feel the need for God after that. I became more interested in the universe and a higher power that wasn't necessarily called God. Apart from taking His name in vain, God and I didn't hang out together. I was too into the planets and the Greek and Roman pantheon to think about one measly God. Plus, God wasn't cool. He definitely wasn't rock 'n' roll. He was all about Jesus sandals, 'Kum ba ya' and people like Cliff Richard. I preferred to find more esoteric routes to divinity. As well as astrology, I dabbled in Rosicrucianism, the spiritual aspects of Jungian psychotherapy and goddess wisdom. Anything to get away from boring old Him. I even mourned my lost connection to my Jewish ancestry, wondering what my life might have been like had I been part of the Jewish community.

It took the intervention of a spiritual midwife to shift my perspective. I enlisted her help and support while I was going through the trials of midlife. She would freely talk about God and guru, while I minded my language. One day she challenged me and I admitted, 'I have a problem with God.' And she replied, 'OK, but then God will have a problem with you.' I continued, chastened, 'Maybe it's just that I have a problem with the word God.' She said, 'Fine. Call Him anything you like – Bert, Charlie, Shed – He won't care. As long as you keep your mind focused on Him.' This was a revelation. I didn't have to call Him God? Wow. Then maybe I'll call him Aragorn – my favourite character in *The Lord of the Rings*. I toyed with that idea for a while but it seemed a little impractical. So, I stuck with God. The idea that I might be severing my connection with the divine simply by rejecting the word God struck me as rather foolish, so I let God back into my life and vocabulary.

Since then, me and Him have been getting along fine. I pray to Him every day. I don't talk about Him that much, though. In fact, this is the first time I've written about

Him at all. My spiritual life and practice are of no interest to anyone but Him. I hope He is amused by the fact that I'm honouring Him with capitalised pronouns. I think that might tickle Him pink, given that I was once His problem child.

The word has a complex history but was originally a gender neutral term that shifted to the masculine with the coming of Christianity. It became God to differentiate Him from all the other heathen gods out there. So, God, whether you're actually a She, not a He, or even a They – I'm sorry. I was sad. I was angry. But I know you will forgive me unconditionally and I hope you'll accept the honour of being my final wise word.

Pause for reflection

Every story needs a satisfying and cathartic resolution. At the end of this chapter I've made peace with what happened to my dad on April Fools' Day 1973 and ended with a tribute to the ultimate father figure – God. Surrendering to the divine hasn't been easy for me. After Dad's stroke, my mum was angry with God, just like I was. There was a lot of resistance to punch through – a lot of 'Why Dad? Why us?' and 'It's not fair', not to mention 'What would my life have been like had he not had the stroke?' I've imagined that life and even wrote a story about it. I was taken aback that this fictional life with a normal, healthy dad turned out to be much less interesting than the life I've actually lived.

What's your resolution story? What transformation did you eventually undergo when you resolved the conflict triggered by your inciting incident? What do your wise words tell you about your life so far?

Wherever you are in your 'story so far', here are some prompts that might inspire you. If it appeals to you, burn some incense while you're doing this exercise or at least find a tranquil space indoors or outdoors that will evoke a feeling of inner serenity. This stage of a narrative is sometimes called 'bringing home the treasure'. In answering one or more of these questions, focus on the wisdom of your life experiences to date. What do others need to know about the lessons you've learned so far? As before, take a pen and allow a stream of words to flow onto the page until you're satisfied with your answers.

- Which words have helped to resolve your story so far?
- Which words describe your biggest transformation?
- Which words still cause you pain?
- Which words have helped you to heal?
- Which words have taught you the most?
- Which words have helped you make sense of your life?
- Which words have carved your soul?
- Which words have connected you to a deeper sense of purpose and meaning?

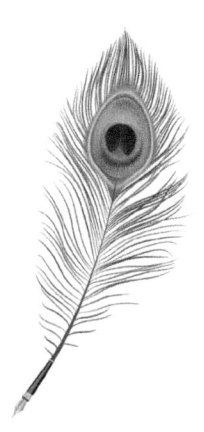

Chapter 7
Last words

As I mentioned before, we're all unreliable narrators – but when we reach the end of life and must hand over the narration to our nearest and dearest, the levels of inaccuracy can go off the scale. I'm sure some of the last words spoken by the famous and notable were genuinely their final utterances; others were no doubt wishful thinking on the part of those tasked with recording history. However, we remain fascinated by last words. A dying Charlie Chaplin allegedly uttered my current favourites. When a priest was reading the last rites and said, 'May God have mercy on your soul,' he's said to have replied, 'Why not? After all, it belongs to Him.' Oh to be that quick witted at the final curtain. Still, it seems unlikely that many of these famous last words were uttered immediately before the final breath.

I was fascinated to discover that a linguist called Lisa Smartt faithfully recorded what her father said in the days leading up to his death. This led her to launch the Final Words Project, which records what she calls 'words at the threshold'. She discovered language patterns that were unique to the end of life, such as repetition, non-referential language (ie words that make unclear or inexplicable references), strange but strangely meaningful statements ('there is so much so in sorrow') and metaphor. Apparently, in our final days, we often speak in symbols and metaphors that were meaningful to us during our lives. Smartt found that common metaphors were those relating to travel or journeys: 'The suitcase is packed. I have to go.' And my favourite: 'The yellow bus is coming! It's filled with angels!' There's something incredibly poignant about these journey metaphors. They fit so beautifully into the universal narrative structure known as the hero's journey, which is a cycle that keeps repeating. Once you have reached the journey's end and brought home the treasure, you begin another journey. To me that dovetails with the Buddhist idea of reincarnation – a journey of birth, death and rebirth that doesn't end until you reach enlightenment.

I can't plan my last words but if I could, what would I say? It obviously depends on the circumstances but if I had all my faculties in working order, maybe it would be something like 'Words have never failed me… but there's always a first time.' I'm happier with the idea that I will be talking in metaphor or gibberish. Maybe I'll speak in dream language, which rarely makes sense. (For example, from one of my recent dreams: 'It's great that a baby has foliage – it shows their connection to Mother Earth.') Where does language go when we die? Will my soul think in words? These are questions I genuinely reflect on. There's a part of me that can't wait to find out, even though 'I' will no longer exist. Is that weird?

When I was writing the first draft of this book, protests and demonstrations were taking place all over the world in response to the murder of George Floyd. I was struck by the way in which protesters used his last words – 'I can't breathe' – as a rallying cry. They took his words and made them powerful. Words do indeed have consequences.

What would you want your last words to be?

Pause for reflection

Taking time to ponder what your last words might be is a strangely uncomfortable but worthwhile exercise, along with identifying the final word on your list.

In a classic story structure, there's often what's called a 'full circle moment' or circular ending which ties together the beginning and ending of a story, with one referencing the other in some way, maybe leaving you with a deeper theme to reflect on. There are numerous examples of this in film and literature. One can be found in *The Lord of the Rings* when Frodo, Sam, Merry and Pippin return to the Shire, where their story started. But they're forever changed by their experience, not least Frodo, who eventually leaves for the Grey Havens, no longer able to live a 'normal' hobbit life.

Does your 'story so far' have a circular ending? Does your final word somehow loop back or connect to your first word? Does it reflect a deeper theme? Mine is simply: words have consequences.

Part 2
How to use your words

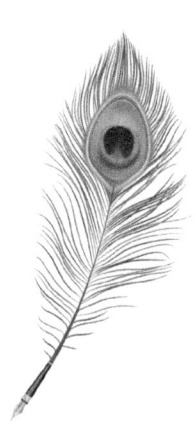

Chapter 8
Putting it all together

Congratulations – you've almost reached the end of your first journey through your life in words. There will no doubt be more. Hopefully, you'll now have a notebook full of the words that have meant the most to you in your life so far – and a collection of lean and meaningful stories inspired by your chosen words as well as your answers to your chosen prompts. So what's next? What can you do with your life dictionary? Here are a few practical ideas and suggested next steps.

If you're a business leader, you could choose a key word story to create a connection and build trust with your clients, customers, team members and other stakeholders. For example, I could use the story I wrote about the word 'shy' to create resonance with someone who was struggling to speak up and have their voice heard. I already use the 'New Romantic' story in some form when I'm introducing myself to a group of delegates on a leadership communications training course and want to establish my credibility and background as an influential music journalist.

In an interview published in the *Harvard Business Review* (Fryer 2003), respected screenwriter Robert McKee says that self-knowledge is the root of all great storytelling and that all great leaders have enormous self-knowledge. 'Great storytellers – and, I suspect, great leaders – see the humanity in others and deal with them in a compassionate yet realistic way.' Showing your humanity and empathy by sharing selected word stories will deepen relationships and give permission for others to share their personal experiences.

Learn from the example of two great leaders who believe in the power of personal storytelling – former US president Barack Obama and entrepreneur Sir Richard Branson. Obama was often referred to as 'America's storyteller-in-chief' and published his memoir, *Dreams from My Father*, in 1995 – before he ran for office as a state senator. He has been quoted as saying, 'I had to know and understand my own story before I could listen to and help other people with theirs.' (Lee 2009) He often used aspects of his diverse and exotic personal story to form bonds with different audiences, build trust and persuade people to adopt his agenda.

Over the course of his lengthy career as a maverick entrepreneur, Sir Richard has often shared personal stories to build trust in himself and the Virgin brand. In fact, he tells the origin story of Virgin Atlantic by recounting the tale of being bumped from a flight from Puerto Rico to the British Virgin Islands to meet the woman who would later become his wife. He ended up chartering a plane to take himself and the other stranded passengers to the BVI for $39 each, jokingly calling it 'Virgin Airlines'. In an article on the Virgin website about storytelling and entrepreneurship (Branson 2016), he says, 'Storytelling is as old as the campfire and as young as a tweet. What moves people is someone who is credible. People can see straight through storytelling that is false, staged or cynical. It has to come from the heart, not just the head.'

If you're a speaker, pick one of your word stories and use it as part of a keynote speech or presentation – or even create an extended version of it for the whole talk. Choose a story that will resonate with your theme and your audience. I often talk about the 'balance of evidence' in a talk – meaning it's important to include emotional content (usually in the form of a story) as well as factual/logical content (in the form of data or research). Scanning through my chosen words, I could tell the story of my professional progression from writer to editor to author; or, for a more personal angle, I could focus on the word 'stroke' and the inciting incident that impacted me for most of my adult life. I could also feature some of my word stories in a talk about words having consequences.

One of my favourite examples of how to use a personal story to deliver a powerful message features in neuroanatomist Jill Bolte Taylor's hugely popular TED talk 'My Stroke of Insight' (2008), in which she relives her experience of having a stroke and shares the profound insights it gave her about the nature of reality. Another is featured in the video 'The Spring', in which Scott Harrison tells the story of his journey from hedonistic nightclub promoter to founder of the organisation 'charity: water' with a mission to solve the world's water crisis (charity: water 2020). It's one of the most profound and moving pieces of storytelling I've ever seen so I can highly recommend watching it. If this video doesn't make you want to donate to the cause, nothing will. It comes as no surprise that what's essentially an ad for a charity has been viewed more than 30 million times. Harrison's 'one word' would, of course, be 'water'. Another might be 'redemption'.

If you're a blogger, you can choose any of your word stories as the theme of a blog. I did it the other way around and was inspired by a blog I wrote in 2013, 'Sole to Soul', to add 'stilettos' to my life dictionary. I now have a resource to help me write a series of blogs with personal themes. I could take any of my word stories and expand them into 800-word blogs with a message and/or lesson that would resonate with my audience. You could also include a word story in a more business-centred blog to add a personal angle and achieve the 'balance of evidence' I mentioned earlier. If you have a word on your list with two different meanings (as I did with 'single' and 'popular'), that will also provide an angle for a fascinating blog.

If you're an author writing a business book, you may find that your word stories can help you illustrate your background, your philosophy of life, your values, your beliefs and your purpose. They can help you connect with your readers, who'll want to know who you are, where you came from and why they should read your book. I often find that the authors I work with shy away from sharing too much about themselves ('I don't want it to be all about me') but as a reader I want to get a sense of the author's personality, their history and life experience in order to get the most out of the information, advice and thought leadership they're sharing with me. If an author has reflected on what's meaningful to them and shared it with me, I'm usually hooked. Elizabeth Gilbert is an author who does this brilliantly – I was just as captivated by her 2015 non-fiction book about creativity, *Big Magic*, as I was by her 2007 memoir *Eat, Pray, Love*.

If you're a midlifer (or you're almost a midlifer) who wants to compile a life dictionary as a form of reflective practice or for personal development reasons, I'd recommend adding journaling to the process. There are no particular rules about how to journal but I can recommend writing 'morning pages' shortly after you wake up every morning. Julia Cameron – author of many books about creativity and writing, including *The Artist's Way* (1992) and *The Right to Write* (1998) – pioneered this technique, which involves writing down anything and everything that comes into your head until you've filled three sides of lined A4 paper. There's no need to hold anything back, as no one else will read these entries. If you find it takes you too long to write three sides, go for two. You can adapt the 'anything goes' rule to write freely and without judgement about particular words you've selected for your life dictionary or to explore your answers to one or more of the prompts in more depth. In the process of writing morning pages (which I've now been doing consistently for two years), I've unearthed some unexpected gems.

I'd also heed the words of Richard Stone in *The Healing Art of Storytelling*: 'As an interpretation, the past can be reinterpreted at any moment. If there is such a thing as freedom, this may be it. No longer must we be a victim of the stories we tell about our past… We can become both a character in our play as well as its author.'

Additional tips

Here's some further guidance for anyone who wants to compile a life dictionary:

- Allow your intuition to guide you at all times – and trust what emerges.
- Once you've chosen some words, write them on sticky notes and put them on a whiteboard or in prominent places so you can continue to reflect on them.
- Make sure these words are the ones that are the most meaningful to you – if not, use a thesaurus to help you identify your precise language.
- To add further depth to your understanding of the words, check their original meaning in an etymological dictionary and see if that shifts your perception.
- If you're a visual person, draw or paint some of your words, as I did with 'surrender'.

As your list emerges, reflect on these questions:

- *Why did you choose these particular words?*
- *What impact did they have on your life?*
- *Why do they still resonate with you?*
- *What meaning do they hold for you now?*
- *Is there energy still trapped in these words that you need to release?*
- *Are these words holding you back from fully living?*
- *Can you make peace with these words?*
- *Can you celebrate the words that have brought beauty into your life?*

- ✎ Can you identify the story these words are trying to tell you?
- ✎ Do these words have a message for you?
- ✎ What are these words trying to communicate?

Responding to these questions and writing about your words will help you process and come to terms with the difficult periods of your life, embrace and acknowledge the painful parts and start to reframe your narrative. This can lead you to writing a cohesive story, identifying each of the key story points in your life so far. See the next section for more guidance on how to achieve this.

Crafting a whole-life narrative

This may prove to be a more challenging exercise but in my experience it's well worth your time and effort. Even though I've explored my life story many times before, I've had plenty of fresh insights while compiling my life dictionary. I'm also struck by the way in which my sequence of words describes the development of my personal and professional identity. I can see the innocence of my childhood words, the confusion in my teenage words, the experimentation in my adult words, the pain and pleasure of my midlife words and the hard-won wisdom of my wise words. Even though there's no obvious connection between some of the words I've chosen, I can still trace a narrative arc.

After completing my life dictionary, I drew a 'word web' on a sheet of A2 paper (rather like a mind map), writing down all my words from first to last. This allowed me to zoom out and see the bigger narrative, which I then read out and recorded. I can highly recommend this as a way of telling a meaningful personal story that hits all the key points in a story structure and also reveals the 'story beneath the story'.

Here's an abridged version of my latest whole-life narrative, with the story structure markers added so you can follow along and create a template for your own story:

The story I'm seeing starts with a lot of comfort, safety, light and laughter. I discover I'm a sensitive child but that sensitivity isn't recognised by everyone around me. At primary school I realise I'm not only popular but also good at writing and singing. I find solace in performing but at the same time feel crushed by some of my teenage experiences. While I'm trying to figure out how I feel and who I am, my dad has a stroke and my life turns upside down [THE INCITING INCIDENT – see page 47].

I start singing with a band, which provides an escape from my confusing emotions. I train to become a secretary and eventually start working for the editor of a music paper. It's there that I begin to develop my talent for writing. I then become a music journalist under a nom de plume. I'm thrust into the pop world of the 1980s, playing my part in the New Romantic movement. I build my reputation as a writer but create a character to hide behind. I'm not really myself because that self is still stuck in teenage confusion. And even talking about it now, I feel sad [PROGRESSIVE COMPLICATIONS – see page 66].

I enjoy career success and even influence the English language. I become a gossip columnist and discover serious dressing up, wearing stilettos and looking like a dominatrix. I project an image of strength to protect my inner core. At the same time I embark on a spiritual quest for meaning and learn about astrology while also entering therapy. I'm emotionally conflicted and can't seem to find

Putting it all together

happiness. Even though I'm successful, I experience many ups and downs.

My professional climb continues: I become an editor but find it too stressful and reach burnout. [FIRST CRISIS POINT – see page 77]. After a period of extreme visibility, I crave invisibility so I fade into the background and ditch my pen name. I reach my peak career years working at national newspapers. I enjoy great camaraderie with my colleagues but drinking alcohol undermines my emotional stability. I enter an extended period where I'm out there trying to enjoy myself but happiness continues to elude me.

I eventually discover toyboy dating and meet my future husband [TURNING POINT – see page 88]. Soon after, I reunite with a dear friend who is terminally ill and dies shortly after. I get married on her birthday the following year. I finally find happiness but, despite the fact that my husband promises to be there forever, the marriage only lasts two years and I have to initiate divorce proceedings [SECOND CRISIS POINT – see page 101].

In my mid-fifties I finally face the grief I've been suppressing since I was 16. I enter a period of deep learning, reflection, healing and solitude. But I also push myself out into the world so that all of those unspoken things start to be spoken about [CLIMAX – see page 118]. I learn how to speak in public and become a coach, trainer and storyteller. I begin to appreciate contentment and serenity and understand the importance of clarity. I become an author. I start to value my intuition and connect to my soul. I reflect on the meaning of surrender and how I've always found it difficult to let go and let God.

That's the story I see here at the moment. The story of

a girl who didn't have the chance to mature emotionally in her teens and early twenties, who tried to become someone she wasn't and went through a lot of emotional and psychological difficulty as a result. But she also took advantage of her opportunities and achieved a lot in her career. While that level of success hasn't been repeated in her intimate relationships, she has reached the point where she's at peace with herself. She feels a sense of calm, comfort and safety through using her intuition and wisdom and her ability to reflect, accept and be grateful for what she has and who she has become. Settling into her elder phase, she's becoming a wise woman who's comfortable in her own skin [RESOLUTION – see page 133].

This is only one of several stories I could write about my life so far but it's one that fits the words I've chosen. I'm still judging myself in some respects so there's another, more empowering story to tell but the resolution gives me a feeling of tranquillity and self-acceptance. It also gives me the sense that I'm the captain of my own life, the author of my own story. I feel as if I've released some of the energy trapped in these words and stories and therefore created more space for myself, psychologically and emotionally. That's the value of this type of reflective work – a deeper self-awareness about the journey so far and a glimpse into where you might be heading next. Using a similar outline, see if you can identify the key turning points and pivotal moments in your story in a way that adds depth and meaning to your experience. Not all of your life events will fall into a neat story structure but I hope you'll benefit from reviewing them and curating the narrative that you share about them.

Superpower word shower

You may wish to compile your life dictionary with the help of a few friends or colleagues. If so, I can highly recommend this exercise (created by Sarah Lloyd-Hughes, CEO of Ginger Leadership Communications and used with her permission), which I often share at the end of group training sessions. A minimum of four people works best.

Each individual, in turn, is 'showered' with words that the rest of the group speak out loud to describe that person's unique qualities and characteristics. Another person writes down the words on a piece of paper (or flip chart).

When everyone has spoken their words (if you're doing it on a videoconferencing platform they can write in the chat), the recipient then reads out the words spoken about them by the other group members and after each word all they're allowed to say is 'thank you'. It's a way of giving people permission to accept affirmation without deflection.

We're not often given the chance to receive affirmation and learn what other people see in us, so this exercise may reveal important words for your life dictionary that may be hidden in plain sight.

I'm including the word shower given to me during one of Ginger's trainer huddles. It's worth keeping your word shower for those moments when you feel sad, anxious or lack confidence. It demonstrates words at their most powerful – as glorious and meaningful gifts:

Beautiful, brainy, calm, caring, clever, compassionate, creative, delightful, friend, fun, funny, generous, genius, insightful, kind, laser-focused, loving, magical, magician, ninja, patient, razor-sharp, sassy, spacious, strong, supportive, vibrant, wise, wordsmith.

Thank you, thank you, thank you.

Epilogue

As you reach the end of this journey through your life in words, I hope you've uncovered valuable insights that will not only help you to live a more fulfilling life but also help others do the same. I hope you go on to tell some or all of your story in a way that's of service to your personal development and your chosen audience. I hope that in sharing my stories I've shown you how you might share yours. I also hope you'll continue to update your life dictionary and build your self-knowledge.

And finally, remember that by choosing your significant words, you'll unearth parts of yourself that have been suppressed, hidden, unrecognised, distorted and excluded as well as parts of yourself that need to be expressed, made visible, recognised, clarified and celebrated. You could say that life is like a crossword puzzle: the right words will help you solve it.

If you're looking for further inspiration to help you compile your life dictionary and explore your word stories, visit beverleyglick. com. If you're seeking support to help you put together a whole-life narrative, please contact me at info@beverleyglick.com

Acknowledgements

First of all, I'd like to thank my friend, mentor and collaborator Nick Williams, who challenged me to draft the outline for this book and then agreed to write the foreword. I encouraged him to compile his meaningful personal stories into a book (*Pivotal Moments*) – and now he has inspired me to do the same.

Thanks to my mum and dad, whose hard work throughout their lives provided me with the inheritance to fund this book – and without whom I wouldn't have a story.

Thanks to my brother, Bryan (the novelist of the family), for his enduring support and literary insight; and my sister, Ginette, for her courage in sharing her story at The Story Party.

Thanks to my dear friends Rona Steinberg, who kindly read an early draft and encouraged me to write more, and Nicky Moran, for hosting her pandemic-era Passion Project programme, which pushed me to finish my first full draft.

Thanks to my colleagues at The Right Book Company, especially Sue Richardson, for giving me the opportunity to do the work I love and believing in me and my book; Paul East, for his marketing and publishing brilliance; and my editors, Marian Olney, for her gentle guidance and insight, and Andrew Chapman, for his eagle eye and encouragement.

Thanks to Sarah Lloyd-Hughes for believing in me as a leadership communications trainer and giving me permission to share the superpower word shower. And finally, thanks to my Story Party collaborators Mary Ann Clements, Yang-May Ooi, Robin Bayley and Jojo Thomas for their friendship and sharing my passion for storytelling.

Resources

Foreword
Williams, N (2010) *The Work We Were Born to Do: Find the work you love, love the work you do.* Balloon View.
Williams, N (2015) *Pivotal Moments: Stories of courage and vulnerability on my journey of doing what I was born to do.* Amazon Kindle.

Introduction
Glick, B (23 March 2020) 'A new language for a new reality'. URL: beverleyglick.com/written-word/a-new-language-for-a-new-reality
Baldwin, C (2007) *Storycatcher: Making sense of our lives through the power and practice of story.* New World Library.
Rogers, C R (1995, first published 1961) *On Becoming a Person: A therapist's view of psychotherapy.* Houghton Mifflin.
Golden, J (2017) *Retellable: How your essential stories unlock power and purpose.* Walkingstar Studios.
Widrich, L (2012) 'The science of storytelling: What listening to a story does to our brains'. *Buffer* 29 November. URL: buffer.com/resources/science-of-storytelling-why-telling-a-story-is-the-most-powerful-way-to-activate-our-brains
Glick, B (2022) 'Leveraging the science of storytelling'. Ginger Leadership Communications 14 December. URL: gingerleadershipcomms.com/article/win-hearts-and-minds-in-turbulent-times-by-leveraging-the-science-of-storytelling
Stanford Business (2021) 'Brains Love Stories: How leveraging neuroscience can capture people's emotions'. Stanford Graduate School of Business, 2 September. URL: gsb.stanford.edu/insights/brains-love-stories-how-leveraging-neuroscience-can-capture-peoples-emotions
Peterson, L (2017) 'The science behind the art of storytelling'. Harvard Business Publishing, 14 November. URL: harvardbusiness.org/the-science-behind-the-art-of-storytelling

Aaker, J (2019) 'Harnessing the power of stories'. Stanford University. URL: womensleadership.stanford.edu/resources/voice-influence/harnessing-power-stories

Mufarech, A (2022) 'The stories we tell about ourselves: Understanding our personal narratives with psychologist Dan McAdams'. North by Northwestern, 25 January. URL: northbynorthwestern.com/the-stories-we-tell-about-ourselves

Gotschall, J (2013) *The Storytelling Animal: How stories make us human*. Mariner Books.

The Story Party: thestoryparty.co.uk

Stone, R (1996) *The Healing Art of Storytelling: A sacred journey of personal discovery*. Authors Choice Press/iUniverse Inc.

Reedsy (8 August 2022) 'Story structure: 7 narrative structures all writers should know'. URL: blog.reedsy.com/guide/story-structure

Reedsy (8 October 2021) 'The Inciting Incident: Definition, examples & writing tips'. URL: blog.reedsy.com/inciting-incident

Online Etymology Dictionary: etymonline.com

Michelson Foy, G (2022) 'The creative benefits of writing longhand'. *Psychology Today* 30 May. URL: psychologytoday.com/gb/blog/shut-and-listen/202205/the-creative-benefits-writing-longhand

Chapter 1

Barley, N (2012) *The Innocent Anthropologist: Notes from a mud hut*. Eland Publishing.

Erard, M (2019) 'A cultural history of first words'. *Paris Review* 26 July. URL: theparisreview.org/blog/2019/07/26/a-cultural-history-of-first-words

Chapter 2

Buster, B (2013) *Do Story: How to tell your story so the world listens*. Do Books.

INFJ personality type: 16personalities.com/infj-personality

Whyte, D (2014) *Consolations: The solace, nourishment and underlying meaning of everyday words*. Canongate.

Goldschneider, G & Eiffers, J (1994) *The Secret Language of Birthdays*. E P Dutton.

Margolis, M (2009) *Believe Me: A storytelling manifesto for change-makers and innovators*. Get Storied Press.

Chapter 3

Story Grid (2023) 'Inciting incident: Definition and 6 examples for how to start your story'. URL: storygrid.com/inciting-incident

Lloyd, C (2023) *You Are Not Alone: From the creator and host of Griefcast*. Bloomsbury Tonic.

Tennis Shoes tribute site: stewartdmv.co.uk/TennisShoes%2002a.html

Chapter 4

Glick, B (4 August 2021) 'Dear Alan, you changed my life. I hope I can be the Alan in someone else's life'. URL: beverleyglick.com/mystories/dear-alan-you-changed-my-life-i-hope-i-can-be-the-alan-in-someone-elses-life

Kemp, G (2009) *I Know This Much: From Soho to Spandau*. Fourth Estate.

Rock's Back Pages (library of music journalism featuring articles by Betty Page): rocksbackpages.com

BBC Radio 4 (2022) 'Gossip: Eight reasons why we can't resist it'. *Woman's Hour*. URL: bbc.co.uk/programmes/articles/5RlZLd0rLY-DztQM5S6zXTLZ/gossip-eight-reasons-why-we-can-t-resist-it

Story Grid, 'Turning point progressive complication: connecting the reader to the protagonist'. URL: storygrid.com/turning-point-progressive-complication

Chapter 5

King, S (1986) 'Everything you need to know about writing successfully – in ten minutes'. *The Writer*.

Toyboy Warehouse: toyboywarehouse.com

Klein, J (2022) 'Dry Dating: The rise of sober love and sex'. BBC 11 February. URL: bbc.com/worklife/article/20220209-dry-dating-the-rise-of-sober-love-and-sex

Glick, B (2009) 'I found my true love at 50'. *Sunday Express* 4 January. URL: express.co.uk/expressyourself/78337/I-found-my-true-love-at-50

Glick, B (2014) 'How marriage to my toyboy husband (22 years my junior) ended in tears'. *Daily Telegraph* 13 August. URL: telegraph.co.uk/women/womens-life/11030461/Divorce-research-Marriage-to-my-toyboy-husband-ended-in-tears.html

Chowdhury, M R (2019) 'The neuroscience of gratitude and effects on the brain'. *Positive Psychology* 9 April. URL: positivepsychology.com/neuroscience-of-gratitude/#home

Allen, S, PhD (2018) 'The science of gratitude'. Greater Good Science Center. URL: ggsc.berkeley.edu/images/uploads/GGSC-JTF_White_Paper-Gratitude-FINAL.pdf

Glick, B (7 October 2020) 'Dear Mum, here's my final gift of gratitude'. URL: beverleyglick.com/mystories/dear-mum-heres-my-final-gift-of-gratitude

Dalai Lama & Tutu, D (2016) *The Book of Joy: Lasting happiness in a changing world*. Hutchinson.

Chapter 6

Senior, J (2021) 'What Bobby McIlvaine left behind'. *The Atlantic* 9 August. URL: theatlantic.com/magazine/archive/2021/09/twenty-years-gone-911-bobby-mcilvaine/619490. Also available in paperback (2023) *On Grief: Love, loss, memory*. Atlantic Editions.

Murray Parkes, C (1972) *Bereavement: Studies of grief in adult life*. Penguin.

Kessler, D (2019) *Finding Meaning: The sixth stage of grief*. Rider.

Popova, M (2012) 'Susan Sontag on writing'. *The Marginalian* 25 July. URL: themarginalian.org/2012/07/25/susan-sontag-on-writing

Story Grid, 'Story Crisis: Triggering Change in the Protagonist'. URL: storygrid.com/story-crisis

Ginger Leadership Communications: gingerleadershipcomms.com

Glick, B (2015) *Dig for the Story in Your Soul: #StoryWisdom to help you author an authentic life*. Amazon Kindle.

Vanaken, L et al (2021) 'Narrative coherence predicts emotional well-being during the Covid-19 pandemic: A two-year longitudinal study'. *Cognition and Emotion* 36(1). URL: tandfonline.com/doi/full/10.1080/02699931.2021.1902283

Konnikova, M (2012) 'Our storytelling minds: Do we ever really know what's going on inside?'. *Scientific American* 8 March. URL: blogs.

scientificamerican.com/literally-psyched/our-storytelling-minds-do-we-ever-really-know-whats-going-on-inside

Northwestern University (2014) 'How your memory rewrites the past'. *PsyPost* 5 February. URL: psypost.org/2014/02/how-your-memory-rewrites-the-past-22569

Popova, M (2013) 'Neurologist Oliver Sacks on memory, plagiarism and the necessary forgettings of creativity'. *The Marginalian* 4 February. URL: themarginalian.org/2013/02/04/oliver-sacks-on-memory-and-plagiarism

The Daily at the *New York Times. Special Episode: The Latest from Minneapolis* (29 May 2020). URL: nytimes.com/2020/05/29/podcasts/the-daily/george-floyd-minneapolis.html

Overbey, E (2011) 'Nabokov's blue butterflies'. *New Yorker* 26 January. URL: newyorker.com/books/page-turner/nabokovs-blue-butterflies

Bragg, M (2003) *The Adventure of English*. YouTube. URL: youtube.com/playlist?list=PLez3PPtnpncRpf__w_8XWEca2EDv25h3e

Tolle, E (1997) *The Power of Now: A guide to spiritual enlightenment*. New World Library.

Furrah Syed's Art Meets Poetry project: furrahsyedart.com/art-meets-poetry

Chapter 7

Final Words Project: finalwordsproject.org

Chapter 8

Fryer, B (June 2003 interview with Robert McKee) 'Storytelling that moves people'. *Harvard Business Review*. URL: hbr.org/2003/06/storytelling-that-moves-people

Obama, B (1995) *Dreams from My Father: A story of race and inheritance*. Times Books (US).

Lee, Carol E (2009) 'Obama gets personal'. *Politico* 30 March. URL: politico.com/story/2009/03/obama-gets-personal-020636

Branson, R (2016) 'Why entrepreneurs are storytellers'. Virgin 9 February. URL: virgin.com/branson-family/richard-branson-blog/why-entrepreneurs-are-storytellers

Bolte-Taylor, Jill (2008) 'My Stroke of Insight'. URL: ted.com/talks/jill_bolte_taylor_my_stroke_of_insight?language=en

charity: water (2020) *The Spring: The charity: water story* (2020). You Tube. URL: youtube.com/watch?v=bdBG5VO01e0

Glick, B (30 March 2013), 'Sole to Soul'. URL: beverleyglick.com/mystories/sole-to-soul

Gilbert, E (2015) *Big Magic: How to live a creative life, and let go of your fear*; (2007) *Eat Pray Love: One woman's search for everything.* Bloomsbury Publishing.

Cameron, J (1992) *The Artist's Way: A course in recovering and discovering your creative self.* Pan Books; (1998) *The Right to Write: An invitation and initiation into the writing life.* Hay House UK.

Storytelling websites and further reading

Story structures: Storygrid.com; blog.reedsy.com

Narrative transformation (Michael Margolis): storiedinc.com

TED talks about storytelling ted.com/topics/storytelling

Bowles, M et al (2022) *How to Tell a Story: The essential guide to memorable storytelling from The Moth.* Short Books.

Haven, K (2007) *Story Proof: The science behind the startling power of story.* Libraries Unlimited.

Metzger, D (1993) *Writing for Your Life: Discovering the story of your life's journey.* Harper One.

Perry, P (2012) *How to Stay Sane: The art of revising your inner storytelling.* Macmillan.

Sachs, J (2012) *Winning the Story Wars: Why those who tell (and live) the best stories will rule the future.* Harvard Business Review Press.

Storr, W (2019) *The Science of Storytelling: Why stories make us human and how to tell them better.* HarperCollins.